How the Land Lies

How the Land Lies

of longing and belonging

Pat White

Victoria University Press

TE WHARE WĀNANGA O TE ŪPOKO O TE IKA A MĀUI

VICTORIA
UNIVERSITY OF WELLINGTON

VICTORIA UNIVERSITY PRESS
Victoria University of Wellington
PO Box 600 Wellington
victoria.ac.nz/vup

National Library of New Zealand Cataloguing-in-Publication Data

White, Pat, 1944-
How the land lies : of longing and belonging / Pat White.
ISBN 978-0-86473-638-3
1. White, Pat, 1944- 2. Poets, New Zealand—Biography.
I. Title.
NZ821.2—dc 22

Published with the assistance of a grant from

creative
nz
ARTS COUNCIL OF NEW ZEALAND *TOI AOTEAROA*

Printed by Astra Print, Wellington

Contents

Places remember events

Our place is being battered by wind this morning. Severe nor'west gales shake the house on its foundations. Trees we have planted bend and dance then stand straight and tremble in aftershock between each gust. The forecasters predict the gales will ease later in the day, before returning from the south tomorrow. Possibly the Rimutaka road is closed. The Tararua range across the valley is silhouetted, arched by clouds, which have their own intense, wind-sculpted and shifting landscape.

Before coming to live here, Catherine and I cycled for months of 1990 through Italy, Switzerland, France, and then up the west coast of Ireland. We pedalled our way through some rough weather at times, but nothing was quite like the north Atlantic gale that hit us near the Cliffs of Moher in western Ireland. I got blown off my bike. Turning my parka into a sail, a gust of wind somersaulted me over the handlebars landing me on my back in the middle of the road. There was nothing between us and the North Pole to soften that particular storm. Two hundred metres beneath the cliffs the Atlantic beat against the rocky shore, huge breakers spraying far inland, smearing windows more than a kilometre from the beach with salt. The sense of that place, Moher, the beach at Doolin and the Aran Islands offshore, in my mind has a wildness touched with a feeling of being at the edge of the world. Men and women crofting there, with stone cottages for shelter, must have been tough, and in the face of the brutal reality of starvation had the survival skills to uproot and sail to distant corners of the earth in the nineteenth century. Some of my ancestors came from Enniskillen in Ireland, but the Scottish branch of the family lived on Islay, another western island territory whose experience is conditioned by Atlantic moods.

In contrast, here our place sits within a landscape as John Stilgoe would use the word: '[landscape as] essentially rural, essentially the product of tradition'. It is also stunningly picturesque at times. Pakeha families, particularly of Scottish descent, within this district have occupied the space as farmland for as many as five generations. Before that, Maori were settled here, and their marae and urupa are still in use. A last remnant of kahikatea bush at Carter's Reserve gives an idea of what much of the district could have looked like. In low-lying areas, or gully sites, creeks would have been host to flax and raupo swamp, before vegetation changed to bush cover on slopes rising to terrace land. The place I have arrived at is Gladstone.

This is where I tentatively locate myself in the world. Although I didn't know it until some years after my arrival, the three acres I live on now are only a half-hour drive from Whakataki where my other Scottish forebears, the Dunn family, started out as immigrants in 1876. I also did not know that my great-grandfather and grandfather had owned land in the district, one at Whakataki and the other at Whareama. These discoveries allowed a deeper, more personal connection to develop.

The first of that family to arrive from Glasgow were John and his sister Jean, who settled at Castlepoint in 1874. John, only twenty-two years old, was kicked by a horse and killed there in 1876 while working as a blacksmith. John's brother, Mathew, with wife Sarah, arrived at Castlepoint from Glasgow a few days after the accident. It would have been their task to organise the headstone, which now lies broken in the Settlers' Cemetery just back from the beach at the town's entrance.

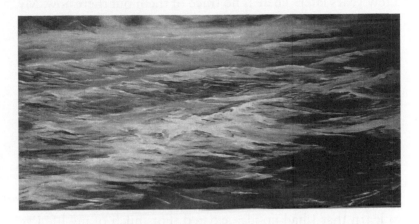

Their own emigration, on board the ship *Waimea*, had already suffered tragedy. Two days from Port Nicholson, after months of sailing, they lost their infant sons within twenty-four hours: Robert, the baby, died from pneumonia, and John, aged two, died from inflammation of the brain. The boys were buried at sea off Castlepoint. When Mathew and Sarah subsequently bought a farm at Whakataki, they were living close enough to stormy seas to hear surf breaking against the offshore reefs of Mataikona—the same seas that contained the bodies of their first-born sons. They worked hard, and raised five more children. In 1890 when their fourth son was born, he was christened with the names John Robert in his dead brothers' memory, and known from then on as Jack. His sister Agnes became my grandmother. In time her son, my father, would be called Jack in memory of his favourite uncle, John Robert.

Agnes married Fred White, one of four brothers from

Hampden who worked on the farms of eastern Wairarapa when they were young; another of the brothers married Agnes's sister Elizabeth. Fred leased farmland at Whareama before the First World War, and his brother owned a farm just down the road but had to sell up because of health problems a few years later. There is no trace of them out there now. My father went to Whareama School for a short time about 1913 or 1914 until the family shifted away from the Wairarapa after Agnes became terrified by a spate of earthquakes. Dad tells the story of arriving home after school to find her sitting on the doorstep, afraid to be inside the house in case there was another shake. He then spent the rest of his childhood in the small North Otago village of Hampden where his paternal grandparents lived.

I have been told a Maori name for this area is Waitoheariki, which can be translated as 'the place of many underground streams'. In the Wairarapa there were personal stories for me to learn that I had no idea existed. For much of my life I've struggled to stay in one place. Yet, staying put has allowed the stories to be partially teased into the light of day. When Maori talk of underground streams, they are not just dealing with the accuracy required by geography, but also the stories of this place. Each stream teased into light, every unearthed strand, has altered the story I live in.

Ross: the railway row

My earliest connections with the world were made in railway towns. During my childhood we shifted from one railway housing settlement to another: Tapanui, Gore, Inangahua Junction, Rangiora, Ross. From Ross we moved to the North Island, where the same pattern occurred. By the time I left my parents' home I'd had enough of railway settlements. Yet, here I am at Gladstone, Wairarapa.

At Gladstone, there are fascinating 'what if' questions. Gazetted in 1870 after being surveyed, the speculator's vision of a township failed to become a reality. The railway line was planted along the west side of the Wairarapa plain, probably for political reasons, and Gladstone township became a sorry little plan on a piece of paper stored under a bureaucrat's desk. What was once someone's dream virtually faded off the map.

My first memories are of living right beside a railway track at Inangahua Junction. But the first place to take on shape and form, if I look back, would be Ross. A railway settlement, as was the case for many New Zealanders, played a large part in how I was formed. Given that New Zealand Railways employed 25,000 staff at one time, there are many children of railway employees living all over the place away from their rural roots. Years ago it was one of my dinner-party tricks

11

among well-off middle-class men and women discussing their sabbaticals, and papers they were working on for this conference, or plans for that overseas holiday, to start talking about the railways. One notable evening, five out of eight of us at the table had railway affiliations from childhood.

These days, railways are a nostalgic relic of the past for many people, a way of life enshrined in songs in which singers such as Australian Frank Ifield strain to capture romance in song lines such as—

I guess the sound of the outward bound
Made me a slave to his wandering ways.

Certainly the days of steam trains are well encapsulated in American blues and country music. Woody Guthrie, Hank Williams, Pete Seeger, Johnny Cash—plus a host of others—followed 'the lonesome whistle', blowing them onto the stage and fame. It was in railway houses, built close enough to the tracks to cause shaking when the trains rolled past, that I first heard country and western songs—a coal range burning, electric lights shining over a room crowded with seven children and tired parents while we read, played cards, did jigsaws or made things out of plasticine. In the 1950s there was memory of depression and war among adults and older children that gave a touch of authenticity to the singers' words. They had been through the hard times, and we'd listen to request sessions on a crackling radio, often in places that had poor or variable reception.

For decades my family lived close enough to the tracks to be woken by the steam train whistle blowing around the same time every day. As children at Ross, we kept time by knowing what train or railcar had come or gone. Some still mornings now at Gladstone, we can hear the train picking up speed across the valley, gathering commuters on an early morning run into Wellington city.

12

There were seven kids in our family, and during the years I was at primary school we lived in a number of three-bedroomed railway cottages. Before Mum got worn out with the shifting, and probably tired of dealing with the demands of a gaggle of so many bodies in such a small space, she had a particular song for each of us to be sung at bedtime on special occasions. Or so the family story has it, but I can't imagine her having time to spend with each one of us in turn, particularly at bedtime. Yet, I do remember once, Mum sitting on my bed one night and singing to me at Inangahua.

Down in the valley
Valley so low
Late in the evening
Hear the train blow
Hear the train blow, love
Hear the train blow
Late in the evening
Hear the train blow

I have no memory of her ever singing to me like that again. I would have been about four. 'Val had a wonderful full voice,' Dad told me more than once after she died.

We grew up with songs in the house, but Mum sang less as we grew older. I don't remember there being much to sing about for people like my mother in places like Ross.

She must have struggled to find room for herself in a house full of children day in and day out. It was, in the 1950s, not far removed from the original raw settlement of 1909—one more railway line laid with dreams of prosperity in every piece of steel track dog-spiked across the countless silver pine sleepers that tied the vision to the ground it traversed, a landscape of swamp and bush.

The type of land that blighted large areas of the Coast was known as pakihi, a bog formed over an iron pan that resisted drainage. It looked abused and unlovable once the bush was cut off it, a wilderness of stumps and scrub, and desolate. A photograph taken in 1909 graphically demonstrates the raw, rough-edged surroundings. This place is the end of the line literally, and for some, metaphorically as well. The camera lens looks north toward the Totara River Bridge and the township of Hokitika thirty-four kilometres away. Just out of sight, two or three kilometres to the east, would have been the township of Ross. Westward was the Tasman Sea, which could be heard pounding into the beach when a big sea was running. At the time of the photograph the great West Coast gold rush had occurred less than fifty years earlier, when Ross had been a boom town of digging claims, sluices and shafts descending below the surface of the hills. To the south there would have been native forest, mountainous country and big fast-flowing rivers prone to flooding. The goods shed, probably painted red, is to the viewer's left; in

Railway Station at Ross, shortly before the line was opened (ca 1909). E.J.M. McClure Collection; Alexander Turnbull Library.

the middle distance, the loco shed and water tower wait for their working lives to begin; and to the right is the station building, almost certainly painted red as well. A row of identical railway workers' houses with their red corrugated iron roofs occupies an area just beyond the station.

The whole shebang was clustered into an area more or less cut out of bush, with flax swamp and scrubby gorse along the back of the houses, crowding their back fences. The railways department housed their workers like that, close to the stations. Many of their staff didn't own cars. They relied on passenger trains, just as we did. Dad never owned a car during his forty years with New Zealand Railways. Among my early memories are train trips, particularly those taken for Dad's latest transfer to a new job, like the one we took to Ross when I was seven years old. I remember that while Dad went off to work, Mum would settle the family into the new house, with efficiency born of practice.

Railway cottages can still be seen in many small towns the length and breadth of the country and have developed a nostalgic charm that can make them sought after as real estate items in some places. Their single identifying characteristic is the little paling-clad porch behind which the front door opens to a passage way, with three bedrooms, then a dining/living room and kitchen at the back. Both laundry and toilet were external. I can remember Dad having to bury the contents of the can that served as the toilet receptacle.

In the tiniest settlements, like Ross, the houses being built at the same time as the station were lined up along the track with little more than a narrow road between front yard and train traffic. Any worker's wife of the era before the purchase of diesel engines would be able to tell you how washing hung out to dry could be ruined if steam engines arrived with the wind blowing the wrong way.

'Get that washing off the line,' Mum would call urgently, every so often when some distraction meant the steam train was on its way and Mum's clean wash was still on the line. It would be a scramble then, to bundle sheets, shirts and sundries into the clothes basket, before the goods train trundled in billowing coal smoke over everything in sight. Soot and coal dust were facts of life for the housewife trying to raise a family in a railway row. So was competition to get the washing hung out earliest on washday mornings.

The laundry was a shed outside which held a copper and scrubbing board. To wash meant lighting a fire under the copper, heating water, hand-winding the finished wash through the wringer, rinsing in separate tubs and wringing again, and the whole palaver once a week. With seven children to care for, the task of keeping clothes clean must have been monumental, without even thinking about cooking and cleaning.

Each house also had a drying rack attached to the ceiling in front of the coal range. Wet washing drying inside was another chore for Mum in this place where rainfall was often over 2500 mm a year, with as many as 160 days or more being wet.

The thing to make a West Coaster homesick is the sound of rain on a corrugated iron roof. 'That is the sound I went to sleep by,' they'll say. 'Heavy rain falling after dark, I'm back to childhood and warm blankets.'

If they lived in a house with a drying rack, as many did, there is also the smell of damp clothing, wet wool, suspended above the mat in front of the kitchen stove—and a line of raincoats on hooks in the back porch, hanging above a selection of gumboots.

The railway row, just like a milling settlement or any small farming valley with its no exit road, could get a touch claustrophobic. The men worked together all week, while the women clustered in houses crowded with kids, getting their kicks out of being first to have washing pegged to the clothesline. There can be a lot of looking over the fence in these places. Mum and Dad bought the *Truth*, a New Zealand equivalent of the British tabloid. Back then divorces were published in this thing each week, and I seem to remember once or twice they knew the recipients of instant notoriety.

'By Jove,' Dad would announce, looking up from the paper. 'Y'know old Fred—well he and Myrtle have divorced.'

'What do you expect?' Mum would say, showing her capacity to judge others' lives. 'I never did think much of him. Too fond of the women by half.' Or whatever dismissive remark it may have been on the day. Tobacco smoke would drift from the roll-your-own cigarette she seemed always to have between her lips, to waft up through her hair, as she bent over the bowl of potatoes, onions or carrots—there were always vegetables to be peeled for dinner. The *Truth* was something to talk about over a cup of tea that was not tangled up with the neighbours. That's the only purpose that sort of gossip rag could serve.

The claustrophobia of living in our neighbours' pockets got at Mum. Net curtains did not always hide the movement of a person who hid behind them while gazing over the neighbour's fence. She resented being looked at by others, feeling they were judging her worth as a mother or housekeeper. Any chance remark could be treated with suspicion, any compliment about what the children were wearing, an idle comment about the garden looking good. So, one evening when my oldest sister lined some of us up along the fence to sing a hit song of the time, 'The eyes of Texas are upon you', while we faced the next-door house, she was happy to laugh at our antics. The net curtains never gave a flicker of acknowledgement, and the incident was not mentioned by any of the neighbours.

We arrived by train to live at Ross in the first weekend of 1952. Dad started work as the stationmaster there on 10 January. Dempsters already lived there. Mrs was tall, and Mr, short. Their boys were Ken, who broke his leg at school playing rugby, and 'Nattery', who was John's age and a real chatterbox, hence the nickname. Clarkes' house was next door to us, with their girls, one of whom was willing to play mothers and fathers until we got into a spot of trouble. When my little brother Chris ran with tattle-tales to Mum, I lied desperately and for once I didn't get a belting. Sandy Seaborn was an engine driver, and others whose names I can't recall lived down the 'row'. Eight or nine houses, dropped along the railway track, about two kilometres from town. Out our front gate in the other direction was the station, and across maybe half a dozen sets of rails where trains shunted and adjusted their wagon conformation were the goods shed and the loco shed where steam trains were turned round to face the other way—and that was it.

In my childhood, two-and-a-half years was quite a stay in one place. As it would not be until 1 June 1954 that we would move on to New Plymouth, Ross is where I spent years seven to ten. Gary Snyder tells us—

> . . . the childhood landscape is learned on foot, and a map is inscribed in the mind—trails and pathways and groves— the mean dog, the cranky old man's house, the pasture with a bull in it—going out wider and farther. All of us carry within us a picture of the terrain that was learned roughly between the ages six and nine.

I had my skull fractured while we were in Gore, following big brother John across the road in front of a motorbike when I was three. Basically, I had to start again from scratch. The railway row at Ross was the first place where I was allowed the chance to discover the world outside the front gate again.

Being fifth out of seven kids was good and bad, though not always in equal shares. At Ross I found out that the four years between older brother John and me was a huge chasm. It had always existed. Dad told the story more than once about the rocking horse at Gore. It was John's but he'd grown too big for it.

'We might have to give that horse a bit of paint,' he said to Mum one day. 'It's time we gave it to Pat.' This was just a standard rocking horse, wooden with metal swingers to provide the rocking of the seat, a budget model countless children will have had passed down from older brothers or sisters. John must have heard them talking.

'Next thing,' Dad tells. 'I went out to the wood heap to saw some wood, and there's John holding the axe. The wreckage of the rocking horse is lying strewn round him.'

Dad asked him, 'What'd you do that for?'

'He's not getting my *buddy* horse,' was John's defiant stand.

A four-year gap meant I was the oldest of the younger lot—but as long as the older ones were round, it was well down the pecking order for me. In a fair swag of situations it made more sense to just shut up and keep your head down, staying out of the firing line. John could wrestle me to the ground, using weight and strength I wouldn't gain for years. Once he had me cornered, the pleasure was in provoking me, tormenting and teasing until I squawked or was in tears.

When he went possum trapping or off with the other older mob to play in the bamboo growing down past the yards—and who knows what games were played in there—part of the pleasure was in making sure I knew he wouldn't let me go with him. I got used to my own company pretty early. Even in a crowded house I learned ways to be out of sight while still in the same room. Keep quiet, keep busy, keep off centre stage, are lessons learned in any house where everyone wants more than their share of available space.

We really didn't have room to swing the proverbial cat, and it could all get a bit ratty after a few days' rain. One of the three bedrooms had four bunks in it, and we four boys shared it. There was no personal sense of ownership, not even the smallest surface.

Mum and Dad used to fight every so often, in a fashion that terrified us as small children. But what else could be expected, the way we all piled in on top of each other? Mum also wasn't above using the old 'you wait till your father gets home' line, and then Dad reacted by dealing out summary judgement all round. It was easy to be in trouble by doing nothing more sinister than being in the line of fire.

'Okay, hit me. I'm the worst,' Keith said, walking into one such session. He'd just started school and the fuss was nothing to do with him. It was very funny, but no joke. There just wasn't enough space for a family of seven kids, not in that house.

Yet there were good times, evenings doing jigsaws, playing cards, all manner of handcraft things . . . and books. I don't remember a time when books weren't part of life. But in my memories, life outside the house in Ross was much more vivid than what took place inside.

The real world existed beyond the front gate—fishing, visiting the next-door farm at milking, being at school, blackberry picking and so much more. That is where I learned to ride a bike, a horse, and bait a fish hook. Sixty years later, my memories are not of the hundreds of days of rain but of the sense of space down at the beach when the sun was shining on hot sand. The endless summers of books like Arthur Ransome's *Swallows and Amazons* appealed to my imagination, but Ross had real summers.

Sometimes the memories can become just a little skewed, in the marginal bits of day-to-day reality we choose to remember. I can vaguely recall Mum and Dad being upset over the Tangiwai train disaster that occurred on Christmas Eve of 1953. Queen Elizabeth II was on her coronation tour of New Zealand at that time, and the tour included a visit to Hokitika. I guess she walked among the crowds at Hokitika raceway. I assume that could be verified from newspaper reports and photographs. I wasn't there. My memory of the event is that Dad took some of us kids fishing for the day. Meanwhile, the rest of the railway settlement boarded the train and travelled, with other South Westland faithful, to Hokitika. What part Mum had in this display of passive resistance by my father, I have no idea. Did she stay in the house enjoying some peace and quiet on her own for the day? Maybe she went to Hokitika with neighbours.

I phoned one of my sisters to confirm this episode.

'No,' she answered my question. 'I was in Westport when the Queen visited.'

'I thought we went fishing with Dad?'

'Uncle Ross suggested we all go to the beach for the day.'

'Were you at Westport while some of us were at Ross?'

'Umm . . .' Beryl paused. 'I really don't remember.'

'Oh, and that was why I was ringing,' I said to her. 'You're older, you're supposed to remember.'

'Maybe we're both right?'

She is sure that she was in Westport when the Queen visited, and that our Uncle Ross Kirkwood suggested he take all the kids to the beach for the day. After laughter and some general discussion, that's where we left it. I've not phoned my cousins, or any other brothers and sisters to try tracing the story to a tighter conclusion. The story fits as it is either way—we had different childhoods, depending on where we were in the family order. Some of my brothers or sisters could have been visiting the cousins in Westport at the time. With seven of us kids, I can imagine Mum farming some of us out to give herself a break over summer.

Dad was given to a spot of anarchy, telling us as children how he buried his fist in a cop's guts during a riot that took place in Christchurch's Cathedral Square during the Great Depression.

'The bullying bastard,' he used to say. 'He just up and

21

whacked this little guy standing next to me with his truncheon. So I gave him one, as hard as I could.' That was our cue to ask anxiously, 'Did you get arrested?'

'No, the crowd was pushing everywhere and he couldn't get hold of me before I cleared out.'

In those days there were instances of Governors General or VIPs able to spend time touring the country in open cars, driving through town after little town waving to crowds holding Union Jacks. Dad would have none of it. Field Marshall Montgomery travelled on one of those trips after the Second World War finished.

'Y'know when "Monty" drove through Gore after the war, the whole bloody street lined up beside the road across from our place, with their flags and stuff. I just kept digging in the garden, didn't even put my shirt on for the sod,' Dad used to say with some delight. Then, with the inevitable dramatic pause, he'd go on. 'He drove past, and never even looked their way. When I looked up over the handle of my shovel, he smiled and gave me a big wave instead.' The slap of a hand on his thigh, and a cackle of derision that ended in his smoker's cough would follow. It is easy to imagine him being determined not to spend the day paying homage to royalty.

The irony is that 'Monty', as my parents called him, probably thought Dad was a returned soldier who'd had enough of parades. Dad had been passed as medically unfit, even though he was a crack shot and able to keep meat on the table by shooting rabbits all through the war. That judgement was the cause of great bitterness for my father. Two of his brothers and Mum's brothers all did service overseas. He desperately wanted to go. The scene at the medical was just another story of our childhood, rolled out on Anzac Day, polished like an old stone.

His body, with the gall bladder and one rib removed, and a history of pleurisy, would not have been up to the fighting life of front-line troops.

'I could have walked any of those bastards in that room off their feet,' he'd declare, before lighting a cigarette and disappearing to the garden where he could brood in peace. 'And I was a better shot,' would be his parting jibe. It was a humiliation to be assessed Grade four. He was in denial.

Dad would tell how, on a day that was freezing, a big barrel-chested man, with his clothes off like all of them, had strutted round like a peacock while he waited to be examined. Special scorn was reserved for that individual because his chest expansion was less than that of my scrawny Dad, perhaps proving that his lung capacity was less.

I did hear him depart from that line, but only once. 'I suppose after he did some training he'd have been fit enough,' he conceded. 'Probably only saw five minutes' action before he got shot. The poor bastard.'

As Dad worked in railways, a reserved occupation, and had been assessed as medically unfit, realistically, he was never going to be able to go to war. But for him the facts were not relevant, nor were they part of his story.

'I was on a bus in Gore, and there were women talking loudly about me and another man sitting a bit further back,' Dad told me another time. 'How their men were away fighting. When the bus stopped, the other joker got up to get off—on crutches and one leg.'

It must have been very difficult to be the recipient of a white feather, as Dad was. If he could have, he'd have been overseas 'like a shot'. 'Yes,' Mum would snipe at him. 'You'd have gone over like a shot. You'd have been shot. Great for me,' she'd continue. 'With the children to look after on my own.' Having got his attention, she could deliver the low blow. 'That's how it is anyway I suppose, between you and your fishing.'

With Dad it wasn't all just stories, however. Sometimes he could stop brooding about the opportunities he missed. One day I sat on a log beside him, in the little patch of bush between the 'loco sheds' and the Totara River, just mooching round. He was probably taking me to see if there were any fish running, and decided to stop and roll a smoke.

'You'll have to be very still,' he said. Then with one hand held out, and imitating the high chirpy squeak of the tomtit through tightly pursed lips, he'd succeeded in getting a pair of the tiny black and white birds paying court round his head. Finally, for a moment, one of them landed on his hand, its head bent to one side, shiny eye interrogating the presence of this other creature. In that incident I can recall Dad's stillness, and the patience my quick-tempered father possessed while away from the house and the demands of others. This attentive presence was the same man who could lay any of us across his knee, or over the arm of the sofa, and thrash us, exploding with a tirade of swearing if someone talked too loudly when he was trying to listen to the weather forecast on the radio. At last he rolled his smoke, and we set off to the river.

We had a huge playground. Mum could be pretty volatile, though, if we went along to the river and didn't arrive home right on time, or something unplanned happened, like John going fishing by himself on the beach for the first time. He went walkabout—didn't get home till well after dark.

'And where d'you think you've been?' Not good. Mum didn't go fishing, so she had little sympathy for its seductive, lost-track-of-time allure. I'd already been down to the beach looking, and told Mum I'd seen a log in the water that I initially mistook for John. Probably when John heard that bit of news he thought he owed me one.

Another night Dad went fishing and, swirling the sinker round his head, hit a piece of driftwood so that the lead weight bounced back and knocked him out. He woke up with waves lapping his face. That was another late night arrival home.

'Have you got any idea what time it is?' Mum didn't let

him out on his own for a while after that little episode.

Old Johnny Douglas, who looked like his relation Charlie (Mr Explorer) Douglas, used to pass our house going fishing every day possible, biking from the township with his fishing pole over his shoulder. He'd park his bike by the railway bridge, then trudge along the river bank to wherever the lagoon breached the seawall dunes, sometimes a five-minute walk, at other times a walk of up to an hour over sand. He'd fish the river mouth until the tide changed, before wandering back to bike up the rise to Ross. Johnny's body stooped and a grey beard covered much of his face, which was also shadowed by an old felt hat. While a familiar figure, he was also a mysterious one. Now I wonder if he really was old, or just a solitary man like his famous reclusive forebear Charlie, who preferred to live away from people most of the time.

Railway bridge over the Totara River, north of Ross Station.

The railway bridge, where Johnny parked his bike, had quite a presence. Some of the older kids used to sit in the V timber trusses while a train rumbled over. This highly dangerous game was an elite dare, and if you were caught, big trouble. We were forbidden to walk across the bridge sleepers by Mum, although John used to set gin traps for possums in bush alongside the railway tracks the other side of the river. I don't remember him catching many possums although they must have been prolific. Later on, when I came back in the 1959 summer holidays, I shot a fair few down there. As an adult, possum trapping often featured, and there were times when I have paid for groceries by shooting possums off power poles and out of trees. A friend of mine even named his farm 'Possum Park' because of the numbers of this noxious pest that thrived on his pastures. So, maybe John did trap a few back then and I just don't remember.

And then there was a place in a little patch of bush, a sort of a clearing that I considered mine. You know, 'all children want to crouch in their secret nests,' Seamus Heaney said. My bush was just past the locomotive sheds, where Dad talked to the tomtits that day, and close enough to familiarity for me to build huts out of ponga fern and fallen branches there in the summer. But that sense of nesting, of security, can be lost. With many changes over the years, arriving at Ross township on a tarsealed road from Haast Pass gives me a sense the isolation has gone.

When I lived here, the township still showed comparatively fresh scars from 'old' gold mining. Jim and Dave Thompson who owned the dairy farm used to go down to Ferguson's Bush and cut silver pine fence posts every summer. Stuart and Chapman's timber mill was sited just across the swamp behind our house, about five hundred metres away from the railway station. They used timber cut out of native bush growing to the south. Their skids were set up along the tracks between our houses and the road to the beach. Timber stacks, freshly cut, smelling of sap and sticky with resin, sat on the skids waiting for shipping on railway wagons. Beside the skids were lumps of mutton fat used to grease them so the timber could slide easily onto the railway wagons. Always, round the skids were waxeyes, great flocks of them, as well as other birds. At weekends some of us boys, me and Kenny Dempster or a couple of other kids, could spend hours having competitions to see who could catch the most birds at one go.

We'd prop up one end of an apple box with a forked stick, maybe twenty-five to thirty centimetres high. A length of string would be tied round the stick, and bait such as a piece of bread would be placed inside where the box would fall, and we'd back off to sit and wait with the end of the string in hand. Before long waxeyes or something like starlings would be feeding. We'd wait till the bread was mobbed by scrabbling birds then pull the string, and have panic-stricken birds flapping round inside. Lifting a corner of the box to catch the birds by hand was a whole different story.

While these days it is hard to imagine seeing waxeyes in those numbers, ways of life change for birds just as they do for human populations. It's possible to walk through the bush on Mount Holdsworth here in the Wairarapa for hours on end, and not hear a single bird calling, either indigenous or introduced. The loading skids at Ross were just another part of our world at that time, and waxeyes went with the skids. Across the shunting yard from the skids were the cattle yards.

Periodically, each autumn I suppose, drovers would bring mobs north from South Westland. I didn't know where they came from then, but it was places like Jacobs River and Whataroa, areas farmed by families whose names still resonate with me: Nolans, Fergusons, and others I've forgotten. The cattle were half-wild, left to run on river flats and flood terraces during the year, then mustered for marking and culling every so often. Men on horseback and dogs used to bring them up the road in big herds, to be loaded onto cattle trucks at Ross, before going over to the Addington sale yards or the meat works over the hill. Inevitably there would be lots of noise, dust or mud depending on the weather, as the cattle were driven into the yards then drafted into truck loads. We were not allowed off our section as the mobs swirled into the railway road, dogs barking, stock whips cracking and men shouting. Once they were in the yards, we could sneak out and have a look . . . so long as we acted invisible. Smells of sweat and cattle, the dung and urine of adrenaline-charged beasts in a state of panic at the confusion, and sounds of distressed cows and mismothered calves, and the defiant bellows of belligerent bulls who'd had enough of being harassed, are as much a part of that memory as the sight of the big-muscled beasts swirling round the yards.

Jim and Dave Thompson had the contract to load the drover's cattle onto the railway trucks each year. They farmed land between the railway and the sea. Thompson's place, to a small boy like me, was a self-contained world of paddocks and animals, a sort of parallel universe. It was most often my job to go over in the evening and pick up the stainless steel billy full of milk we bought from them. If I went over early enough after school, I'd be hoisted up-behind on their horse to go get the cows in, sometimes from across the river. Then I'd help get cows into bales and anything else I could do without being in the way. The smell of cows, their cud-chewing placid nature, and the individual characters of the mixed-breed herd enchanted me.

Jim and Dave were just a couple of bachelor farmers, lean and weather-beaten, stooped from the task of milking and endless fencing, with what seemed a natural reticence— yet they were prepared to put up with a young kid tagging along as they went about their daily farm work. I'll always be grateful for that. Dave had been wounded overseas in the war and was unpredictable, while Jim tended to seriousness. Once, Jim put the dogs after me and a couple of other boys when we were chasing some ewes in their crop paddock. It must have been very funny to see, but we didn't stop to look. The dogs didn't know what they were doing really, just barking and running. I was told not to come back till I learned how to behave myself. It wasn't long before I was back there, helping get cows into the bale for them.

Their sister Helen also lived in the big dark farmhouse, which was shaded by tall macrocarpa hedges. She cared for their mother, and for them, and played the organ up at the Presbyterian Church in Ross each Sunday. There was a sense they had enough of the world where they lived, without looking about for other possibilities. There were many small things that added to their environment, making for a way of life that was interesting and changeable. I recall Dave finding a little blue penguin under a shed up near their hay barn, probably about five hundred metres from the sea. The penguin, having travelled to find a quiet possie, probably drew the farm dogs' attention to itself accidentally. They'd have scragged the frightened creature had they been able to get to it hiding under the floor of that shed.

The summer of 1954 was very dry and there was a bush fire burning south of Ross. We could see smoke in the distance for days. That year the ponds on the farm started drying up, and I remember one where the water had dried into a mud puddle in which there were dozens of eels wriggling all over each other making the mud itself appear to be a seething living beast. Newborn calves couldn't be sold, so any that Jim and Dave didn't keep for milking replacements, or that were the wrong breed for beef steers, were killed for dog tucker. I saw calves stunned with the back of an axe before they were killed by having their throats cut. Farming that sort of country, so far from markets, was not for the fainthearted.

Possums were trapped and their skins were dried on

boards in the hayshed, or sometimes tacked to the big swinging doors. The hayshed was a magic place for a small boy, with its harness for the horses, tools and equipment. Horses were still used to work the land. I didn't go much for the smell of possum flesh, or their skins, but the smell of harness leather, with neatsfoot oil rubbed into it, is still evocative of happy times. Another smell dripping with sunny days still remembered is that of mown hay, which was made without a baler and pitchforked from big wagon loads into the loft of the hay barn. This activity was a ritual as much as a job. Loose hay freshly tossed into the loft—it's fun to roll in if you're a kid—and I'm reminded when dried grass is shifted and the sweet smell wafts up, how in those days farmers would pick up a wad of hay and smell it, equating sweetness with quality. And in the barn, we'd raise dust clouds as we moved, so that it would be possible to turn away from the dim interior back to the open door, and see sunlight outside through dust particles—the intricate dancing of countless fairies.

Even wet weather worked for me. Jim or Dave would set off for the cows, astride the horse and wrapped in an oilskin coat, leggings and sou'wester hat. They'd arrive back with the herd, and then there would be the wet coats of cows standing waiting their turn in the yard, steam rising off their flanks, smelling of grass and earth. Fresh milk squirted into stripping buckets after the machine cups were taken off. I was even allowed to take my turn with some of the quiet cows, squeezing teats, hearing the milk flow into the bottom of the metal bucket.

Now, a place like that fronting onto the sea is probably worth a small fortune. Back then, it was just where I went after school. If Mum was mad at me for any reason, punishment was being made to stay home.

I am unable to remember the packing and unpacking for the shift from Rangiora to Ross, but by the time we left Ross I remember clearly the newspaper and tea chests, Mum standing by the container, telling one of us what to bring next from the cupboards, making sure the older ones wrapped each plate, cup or glass the way she showed us before she placed them in the chest, packing extra crumpled paper where it was needed. Then there was the feeling of our belongings being carried by strangers and placed in railway wagons shunted as close to the front door as they could get. Even the grownups' drama of having to get right to the back of the loaded wagon, when Dad discovered his wallet holding the tickets was securely packed away in the wardrobe (which was loaded first of course), did nothing to stop the empty rooms of the little state house we had inhabited echoing as we played in them for the last time. At Ross I had grown into an awareness of living in a particular place. Of course I sometimes wonder what would have happened if Dad had not been so busy chasing promotion . . . if we had stayed on, to grow up in that outdoor wilderness, near the bush and the beach.

A few years after we left Ross, following three other shifts, my father was appointed station master at Greymouth. In a sense we travelled full circle, back from the North Island, where we lived in New Plymouth, Maungaturoto and Rotorua. Fishing again off a West Coast beach, at Blaketown, a suburb of Greymouth, Dad and I discovered a float from a Japanese fishing trawler. We began to see their fishing lights, a faint glow over the horizon after dark, netting huge catches while inside the New Zealand maritime boundaries. In no time the beach fishing deteriorated. Another few years and the railways were sold off by the government.

In the summer of 2008, fifty years later, Catherine and I travelled on holiday through Haast Pass, and called in at Ross to see where I had lived. There is no sign that the railway row had ever existed. The land is still there, growing weeds. A remnant of shingle road winds down to the river, and nothing else: those tracks that followed the contours of the land, travelling south from Hokitika, have been lifted. Where they passed Lake Mahinapua and Ruatapu, across the Totara River to terminate close to the cattle yards and Stuart and Chapman's timber mill, they have become history. From Hokitika a desolation of pakihi swamp, cut over bush and rush- or gorse-infested farmland has been spruced up to appear with 'ten-acre block' prosperity along the tarsealed road. The railcar two of my sisters, Aileen and Beryl, used each day going to high school in Hokitika no longer clatters back and forth. My older brother John joined them on that trip for his third-form year, and he is now ten years dead. The oldest of the girls, Lesley, who nursed at Hokitika hospital, and who used to come home for time off on the same railcar, has long since retired from Stratford Hospital.

We stopped to buy honey from a roadside shop in Ross. A grey haired slightly heavy-built man looked over the counter at me. There was no mistaking who he was.

'You'd be Basil,' I greeted him.

Shaking my hand, he looked hard. 'That's right,' he said. 'But I'd like to know who you are?'

'Pat White. Lived down at the railway settlement.' I could see him thinking. 'It's a fair while ago now. We were in the same class for standard one and two.'

'Oh, you're one of those boys that made all those little models of animals with plasticine . . .', and we laughed. It was fifty-five years since we'd seen each other. For a few minutes we chatted intermittently while he served customers, selling West Coast honey to tourists. He'd worked briefly as an undertaker in Hokitika back in the 1960s before returning home.

'I was the librarian at Hokitika, from sixty-nine until seventy-three,' I told him.

'I didn't even know that.' He paused. 'No, by then I was back here. We were pretty busy for a few years then.' Now he is semi-retired with back trouble from those hard years working the hives. His family runs the business while he just fills in from time to time when they get busy. It was good to see him, to indulge a little nostalgia.

We returned to the car with a couple of pots of bush honey in our hands, to leave without looking back. My childhood, the railway settlement at Ross, were gone.

Way stations

My ex-wife recently carried out an act of thoughtfulness for which I can be very grateful. We separated, in a manner that does neither of us much credit, over thirty years ago, another station along the way. But last year she mailed a parcel to me. This was a most unexpected gesture. Inside the unpretentious carton were wrapped some small ceramic cups and saucers made by an old friend of ours from Westland. A basic shape, salt glazed and with that mottled brown effect one could date back to the 1970s, they were typical of the work Daphne Simpson was producing at the time. She and Frank were our close friends, and among many casualties of shared acquaintance when we separated. Unpacking the little clay objects delighted me, for the tactile quality with which earthenware resonates, and for the memories of the maker they embody.

A couple of other items lay across the bottom of the package. Unwrapped, and seemingly of little importance, were two books, published by Nelson & Sons Ltd, little red hard-covered editions measuring only 15 cm by 11 cm. One was a school prize awarded to J.F. White, dux of Hampden School in 1921.

Inside the cover of the other, written in a hand quite unmistakable to me, was my father's signature, J.F. White,

This is to certify that Mr John Frederick White (Date of Birth 30 June 1908) was employed in the service of the New Zealand Government Railways Department in the following capacities:

Date	Capacity	Location
1. 7.1924	Cadet Telegraph	D.T.M.O. Christchurch
23. 5.1925	Cadet	Dunsandel
12. 9.1925	Cadet	Greymouth
6.10.1925	Cadet	Stillwater
3.11.1928	Cadet	Christchurch Pass
26.11.1930	Clerk	Hawarden
11.12.1931	Clerk Relief	Christchurch Pass
20. 3.1934	Clerk	Invercargill
24. 4.1935	Clerk	Makarewa
11.11.1935	Clerk	Invercargill
26. 1.1937	Clerk	Hampden
31. 1.1941	Clerk Relief	Oamaru
27. 8.1941	Stationmaster	Tapanui
18. 5.1945	Inwards Goods Clerk	Gore
1. 4.1946	Assistant Goods Clerk	Gore
24. 2.1948	Stationmaster	Inangahua
25. 8.1949	Shift Clerk	Rangiora
10. 1.1952	Stationmaster	Ross
1. 6.1954	Claims Clerk	New Plymouth
18. 1.1956	Stationmaster	Maungaturoto
5.12.1956	Asst Stationmaster, Passenger	Rotorua
16.10.1958	Asst Stationmaster, Passenger	Greymouth
5. 4.1961	Chief Stationmaster	Westport
18. 9.1961	Chief Stationmaster	Greymouth
14. 7.1964	Retired on Superannuation	
26. 9.1966	Temporary Clerk	LS&WFO Greymouth
10. 8.1968	Resigned	

I. E. Trask
ACTING GENERAL MANAGER

Per:

Hampden. On the opposite page his signature again, added a year later, J.F. White, Railway Cadet, Christchurch. The writing of his name was given the full flourish, as becomes a young man starting out and testing his sense of self on the page. He bought the book in Hampden, or was given it, then took it with him when he left home to go and work for the Railways Department in Christchurch in 1924. The titles of these little volumes are *Silas Marner* by George

35

Eliot, and *The Vicar of Wakefield* by Oliver Goldsmith. I have no memory of having them in my possession, yet how else would they have ended up with my ex-wife's belongings? Somehow, thirty years earlier, in the hectic shambles of our separation they must have been packed in cartons that left our home with her possessions.

It is something of a fluke that they have survived to be placed on my shelves again, alongside other titles I value highly. An even smaller embossed pseudo-leather-bound volume of *Gems from Longfellow* is also a survivor, though much the worse for wear. Inside that volume, a presentation plate marks the award of First Prize in Form III B at Granity District High School to my mother, Val Kirkwood. She left school before another year was through to work in a fish and chip shop.

Others occupying shelf space beside those from my parents' youth include another miniature edition published by Nelson & Sons, but this time with a blue cover. Francis Bacon's *Essays* I bought from Brislane's Bookshop, on Mawhera Quay in Greymouth, while I was still at school. I also purchased its companion at about the same time, a small blue-covered volume of essays that sits on the shelf beside Bacon. *Essays of Emerson* is an Oxford publication, and shows signs of regular reading along the way. The Miss Brislanes' old-world bookshop on the Quay was an anachronism in this coal-mining and timber-milling region, where fishing boats went out over the bar of the river mouth into hazardous seas and danger, and one's worth was measured by an uncompromising physicality. The Brislanes, two women who seemed old to me, genuinely loved books and had some surprising and very worthy titles on their shelves. Small towns had choice in the 1950s and 1960s, before The Warehouse and PaperPlus flushed the system with remainders, the homogeneous titles of popular culture. In Greymouth, for example, when the Miss Brislanes retired,

Peter Hooper, an author and Thoreauvian philosopher, opened his shop called Walden Books, a name that still resonates with Coasters from that sixties vintage.

Part-time jobs, such as paper rounds, paid for the essays' purchase, or work in the St James picture theatre selling ice creams at half-time during films like *The Greengage Summer*, *G.I. Blues*, *The Nun's Story*, *On the Beach* and *Ben Hur*. I'd rather have been buying an ice cream than selling one, and handing it to some blue-eyed girl with a pony-tail sitting beside me. The idea of asking a girl, with eyes of any colour, to go out to a film was beyond the realms of possibility. The rules of that particular social engagement were unknown to me, and the ability to ask a girl on a date way out of reach. I was far too awkward by a country mile, happier in my own company, yet perpetually longing to be otherwise.

One more volume of essays is worth a mention. MacAulay's *Lays of Ancient Rome: With Selections from the Essays* is a book I must have poozled from the parental bookshelves when I left for Christchurch Teachers' College in 1963. This publishing curiosity hearkened back to a time when books, as this one was, could be 'printed and published for C. Smith, the cash Draper, Cuba Street, Wellington'. What was a healthy sports-playing, girl-hungry teenager doing reading books like that in Greymouth? I am damned if I know. Yet there I was, reading all sorts of things just beyond my comprehension, as well as listening to classical and operatic music to which my background provided no way in. My younger brother Chris had a better handle on things, reading anything that crossed his path—including Plato's *Republic*—while keeping a store of *Man* magazines, with their bikinied or bare-bosomed beauties, well hidden from adult eyes. He even managed to get banished from Rotorua Public Library as a ten-year-old for haunting the photography section of adult books with their nude studies. What I would've given for a dose of that 'devil may care' attitude, or his ability to tell stories of trips down to the lupins and sand dunes with friends, spying on couples seeking privacy.

A selection of books and records had been left at 10 Smith Street, Greymouth—the house my parents bought late in 1958—that reflected the taste of a more educated social class than that of my own family. It was from that collection that we discovered MacAulay and Plato. The once genteel society family home, long inhabited by a now-deceased widow, was left vacant—to be sold as is, where is—full of quality furniture besieged by borer and therefore useless for any role except firewood, bookcases full of books (some hundreds of years old), and a wind-up record player with a generous supply of brittle, easily broken, pre-war twelve-inch 78 rpm records. I listened to all of them, every scratch, crackle and classical note of them. Reading from the shelves in the old house—perhaps a life of Chopin, or Debussy, and, notably, a large biography of Napoleon Bonaparte in which the Moscow retreat is memorably depicted—also occupied many hours.

Not a single floor in the house was anywhere near level due to earthquake damage over the decades, but by far the best thing was that there were plenty of rooms. After living at close quarters in railway houses through our early childhood, for the first time in our lives, my brothers and I were able to get the hell away from each other's space on a wet day. It was here that the habit of reading, which my parents nurtured in all of us, began to absorb my time. Simultaneously we also began to grow apart as brothers—our sisters had left home during the years we lived in the North Island. Each of us boys could easily have been separated by glass, occupying the same space and running parallel lives, unable to reach or get on with each other in any meaningful way. No matter how many times we went to the movies on a Friday night, or fishing with Dad along the shingle bank above the Grey

River Bridge to Cobden, we began to drift off in different directions.

The Greymouth years took their toll on our parents. Mum spent months in hospital with tuberculosis, and looking back I see that she never recovered from that illness—even though the disease itself was cured. Dad spent from April to September of my 6th Form year working in Westport through the week, arriving home on Friday evening often the worse for wear. With my full share of adolescent self-absorption I couldn't get out of town soon enough, leaving for Teachers' College in 1963 with my mother's angst echoing in my ears.

'You'd do anything to get away from here,' she accused.

'You're damned right,' I could have answered, but remained silent. Using a habit that would only lead to trouble down the track, I held my tongue and let my feet do the answering. I learned slowly how damage accrues if our adult ways of responding to common daily events depend on the example of our parents. We need to forge a path of our own. It is seldom wise to just blunder on, doing things the way we do without questioning. Our generation is given to learning after the crash, if we learn at all.

It took forty years to get answers from Dad that would have been bloody handy for me as the doors opened to adulthood. Back then maybe he didn't have a clue either. I've got no way of knowing and thankfully there is no way back.

Dad died aged ninety-one. Two years before he died, I showed up at his house in Stratford with home-brewed stout and a tape recorder. We sat down, had a long talk and a fair bit to drink, and ended up with two sides of a ninety-minute tape filled with his version of the past—his past.

Me: So, by the time you were twenty you'd lost a lot of people . . .
Dad: You're right there.

39

Me: You must have felt if you loved somebody, they'd
       die.
Dad: Yes, that's pretty much how it was.
Me: That's a tough way to live.
Dad: Yes, I suppose it is . . .

After travelling back home I played the tape through once
and put it away, satisfied that a lot of important questions
were answered for me and the family. There would be plenty
of time to check it out later. Next time the cassette wound
through the player it was Christmas and my sons, Andrew
and Gareth, were with us on holiday.

'Listen to this,' I said. Gathered round, in chairs or on
the floor, we heard nothing more than the winding of blank
tape through the speakers. Ninety minutes of information
had disappeared. For a while I puzzled over how that could
happen. In the end, I let it go. How would I know what
occurred? Dad managed once more to slip away without
letting us in on what was really going on.

The transcript written above is possibly accurate, but
more likely an approximation of the conversation we had
over home brew that afternoon. Or was it one morning,
when we sat at the kitchen table and talked? An old friend of
Dad's called in while we were talking. I turned off the tape
and we shared a glass with him. What was the old fellow's
name? I don't remember. Memory is the most approximate
of histories. Yet in our daily lives, it's a primary resource.
God help us! Memory, that elusive beast telling our story,
constructing the myth we spout forth as history, can serve us
ill. If we place too much trust in memory and language, our
imperfection shapes our stories into something manipulated
or elusive. And what's more, our version can live at odds
with the stories of others, who may share similar memories
but from a different perspective.

My father hid behind a mask of yarns pasted into place

with years of practice. The air of conviction, the ability to declaim, holding an audience with his eyes while not really looking at anyone in particular, all contributed in the role of Jack White, storyteller and hard case with a past. Layer after layer of telling perfected his script, and his laughter that accompanied the often-told stories was a punctuation mark, a signature of sorts. A yarn he had told many times, with himself as leading protagonist, I read in one of those five-dollar collections that are published from time to time, *One Hundred Best Yarns from Otago*, or *Best Golfing Stories*. Of course I can't remember the specific incident, so it may just be that I wished from time to time to catch him out. Talk about gullible. He had a way when he was older of turning his hearing aids down if the conversation didn't interest him. Then every so often he'd interrupt, with a heading of sorts. 'Stillwater—' he might say, '1926.' Or it may be, 'I remember the Pomahaka River in 1943. One night . . .', and he'd be off, with a captive audience.

We thought Dad was always talking about himself, and now I can see there were times he was being various, manipulative, or taking us for fools. I reckon he told stories all the time to hide behind them. Well, the technique sure as hell worked. After his death, while he lay in his coffin in the front room of his home awaiting the funeral rites, the same old friend who had visited when I had the tape machine out among bottles of beer came in. He looked down at my father, visibly upset.

'Oh Jack,' he said. 'I'm going to miss your stories.'

Standing in the doorway, I turned away not knowing if I should laugh or cry. My old man, the teller of tales.

He did have some fine stories. There was the one where he arrived home one night wildly drunk. When Dad took to the bottle, which he did only seldom while my brothers and I were of primary school age, it was an act of extravagance. There was vomiting and noise. So one night (in this story) he went out, got drunk, then communed with the toilet bowl, and ended up feeling sorry for himself. At some point, he cried out in his anguish—Dad could always be relied on to make a noise when out of his physical comfort zone.

'Oh Jesus Christ!' he cried. Such a great performance, and of course we were all awake, lying in our beds, blankets round our chins and lights out.

'Oh, Jesus Christ!' he cried out again.

'Yes man,' piped up my youngest brother Keith, who was only eight years old. 'What do you want?'

There was silence for a moment, then next thing we were all laughing. Except Dad of course! Now this is a funny story, but it was Dad who told it against himself years later—after editing. His version suggested he'd hit his thumb with a hammer or some sort of implement, before modestly exclaiming 'Jesus Christ'. I'll stick with the version laced with too much booze, the one with what Australian poet Les Murray would define as 'sprawl'. That story repeated, of a night on the bash, could be one where the teller is prepared to own his failings and faults, recognising that while none of us is perfect, the imperfections are often where we live our lives most vividly.

Another story I, along with my brother Chris, heard only once. We'd asked Dad something personal one day, and maybe it was about why he'd shifted so many times. That was what his reply was about anyway, why he shifted so much. I'm not sure to this day if he realised that when he shifted that meant we all had to.

This is the gist of what he told us. An incident occurred when he was a cadet at Christchurch that put him in hospital for months. He was clowning round with other young men in a swimming pool. Things went horribly wrong. They held him under water too long and he passed out. His mates cleared out and left him in the changing sheds on the concrete floor. When he was discovered by the caretaker he was very ill and had to be taken to hospital. He developed pleurisy.

The result of the escapade was that his seniority of service altered. Two or three hundred other young railway cadets became senior to him, passing exams while he was in hospital. They consequently superseded him, receiving promotions that put them ahead of him when he came back to work.

The short version of this tale concerns his willingness to shift anywhere at any time for years afterwards, and with each shift he clawed back a small fraction of seniority. It is still difficult for me to comprehend the wacky obsessive sense of purpose that allowed him to know with each shift how many men he had overtaken, even as late as his shifting to Greymouth nearly forty years afterwards. His pride in the fact that he overtook all but three of the initial bunch that leapfrogged his seniority was, and is, beyond my understanding. Yet that was the story he told us that day. Our mother and the seven of us kids traipsed round New Zealand living out a grudge match our old man was playing with people who couldn't have cared less—it was all in his mind.

Yet nothing is ever as simple as it seems on the surface. There was a shift being talked about. I remember giving Mum the old 'I don't want to shift' routine.

'Oh well,' she responded, 'your father's decided and that's that. You're going the same as the rest of us.' So that was it, the subject was closed. Later, outside in the garden with Dad, I tried again.

'Why are we shifting?' I asked him.

'Well, y'know,' he replied straightening up, with a fork in hand and his eyes turned towards the house, 'Val isn't happy here. It'll be a lot better if we go.' There was sadness in his voice, a sense of resignation I did not understand, which is probably why the memory sticks.

'What will be better?' I wanted to ask.

43

After all, I was leaving behind friends, sports teams, things I enjoyed like fishing. I had jobs to earn pocket money. Right then in my early teens and on the verge of growing up, it seemed I understood less about being grown up than I ever had. What was going on? For my parents it seemed there was always a good time coming, while the past was a collection of events soured by what they should have done. From stories my sisters tell, it was not always like that. In the long run, shifting was no solution as it left them both exhausted and devoid of roots.

However, there is another story. One my father did not want to tell. In 1919 during the Spanish flu epidemic, in which more people died than during the Great War that immediately preceded it, my father ended up in hospital with a flu relapse and pneumonia complications. He was not expected to live. While he was there struggling for his own life, his father died at home. In the preceding five years he and his family had lost his favourite uncle Jack at Gallipoli, an aunt at Porirua Mental Asylum, a baby sister and, the day after his father's death, an aunt who lived next door at Hampden in North Otago also died of the flu. Dad was only ten, the eldest of five brothers.

After he got out of hospital Dad got involved in a fight in the playground because another boy reckoned Dad's father had committed suicide. Only when he was taken to the headmaster's office was he told that this was in fact the truth. His father killed himself one night while Dad was in hospital. There is a photo taken soon after that occurrence, showing graphically what a toll it took on my ten-year-old father. Dad believed from then until the day he died, that if he hadn't gone into hospital, his father would not have committed suicide.

I was well into my thirties before I was told about that event, and then only through direct questioning of my parents. Of the other deaths and relatives, nothing was learned until my sister Lesley decided to plunge into the revealing world of genealogical research about the time I turned fifty. She was only trying to distract the old man from the distress my mother's death caused him, but the project grew a life of its own. He had no stories to hide behind when he lost his wife, and in his eighties no new job to shift to, taking him away from the face of harsh reality.

No golden-haired child could rescue him, as George Eliot ensured Silas Marner was ultimately rescued by Eppie in that book he had read so many years earlier. In his final years, Dad gradually curled away from us, to some place only he could go, to live out his last story.

Jack White, aged ten years, standing behind his mother Agnes White with his four brothers, shortly after the loss of his father.

When someone takes their own life, the waves spread through the generations that follow with a force that is both surreptitious, because outsiders are unable to understand, and malicious. Questions remain unanswered, simply because the person with the answers is no longer alive. Those who follow on have to do what they can to fend off the darkness of guilt and unknowing which the act invites. Suicide interrogates the living, their getting up each morning to face another day.

My younger brothers and I knew our parents were troubled by something, but we didn't have the answers. Just as I could be relied on to hold my tongue, and a grudge for many years, Chris and Keith were different. Keith would take hurt feelings to his guitar and play another tune, often for hours on end. Chris could be relied on to fight back, no holds barred, if he felt our parents were wrong about something. From my point of view it looked as if he was everlastingly going out of his way for trouble. Yet, there is the story he told me of how it was for him when he was phoned with news of Dad's dying.

'You know how sometimes things flash through your mind,' he said, 'before you can even put words round them? Well, you know what flashed through mine?' he continued. 'I don't have to kill myself now.'

Before daylight

Be careful what you're dreaming
Soon your dreams'll be dreaming you
    Willie Nelson

First the bellowing noise of approaching trouble. Then fetid breath, the rank body smell of bull entering the room. Mayhem! The nightmares start. They were there in my twenties, thirties and didn't fade for another two decades.

With no place to run, I have to hide—in cupboards, behind doors, in the ceiling. And always, always the snarling laughter as another gate is smashed, another wall trashed and the cloven hooves rattle over floor boards.

'You reckon you can hide in there?' Followed by savage bellowing of the enraged beast. 'I'll get you!' And waking. Waking with cold sweats, dry mouth and a heart beating to burst my ribs apart. Once I may have tried going back to sleep, but not anymore. It is a matter of getting out of bed, writing down the dream, putting on some music, making a drink, doing anything rather than return to the blankets and the dark.

Bulls, so much a part of my ordinary farming life during the day, came out of the walls at night frequently enough to challenge my sense of sanity. But it was not memories of escapades with bulls being encapsulated in my dreams. What took place in daylight was never as threatening as that black shape charging out of the dark, night after night. As I would learn over the years, there is no escaping the bull inhabiting my sleep, without some acceptance of the person I am.

What happened at Inangahua Junction was first. I was four, and walking to the township with some of the older kids. We walked a road bordered by a dairy farmer's paddocks, overgrown fences and that sort of thing. In memory a bull is behind us, every time I start to run it trots. If in response to the urging of the others I hold to a walk, so does the bull. I want to run and run.

Inangahua again. A vague flash of rush and fright, picnic things being picked up and people running . . . a bull has jumped the fence.

Ross railway station and cattle loading, ten years later, in the summer of 1959. Mobs from South Westland, Whataroa, Ferguson's Bush and Jacobs River trucked to the yards at Ross. I'm fourteen and 'helping' get stock from trucks to yards to railway wagons. As always there are dogs, shouting men, cows and mismothered calves trying to locate each other, bulls, dust rising over the yards, the smell of diesel . . . and one old bull that is not going down the chute to the yards under any circumstances. Each move he makes shakes the truck—the crash of his flank on the timber sides of the crate as he turns splinters boards. I am asked to distract him while a man drops behind the dividing door in the truck. He will be in position to shut the gate the minute the bull moves into the rear half of the truck again. I lean over the truck side, wave my hat. The enraged beast turns. The man drops behind the door. Infuriated, the bull lunges towards me, bellowing full in my face.

'Jump!' someone yells. In midair, leaping backwards away from the truck, I see his head above the wall of the crate momentarily—then I'm on the ground. The truck shudders once more from the impact of the bull. He looks for anything else to attack—and that is it. There is a split-second chance and the man in the truck swings the door against his rump. The bull is down the race into the yards. I wipe flecks of spittle off my hair.

'Don't be so bloody silly next time!' Dave yells at me, before heading off into the noise and chaos. And a couple of days later I'm home, back at school, getting on with my teenage 'townie' life.

There are other bulls. At Coal Creek I work for a man who milks Friesian cows, and that is where I get chased out of the paddock by a bull one day, while checking the cows. The same bull shoulders me aside at the milking shed gate another afternoon, when I'm trying to draft a mated cow out of his paddock, back in with the herd. No amount of whacking with a stick is going to turn him from the cows in the yard. It is only a few months after leaving that job when I hear the boss has been in hospital after the bull bailed him up one milking and dealt to him.

A year or two later I lease a farm at Blackwater. One morning I decide to shift a young Jersey bull we own. Getting up from the breakfast table I put on my boots and amble out to the paddock behind the house, rolling a smoke as I go. The bull is grazing quietly. As I approach he lifts his head, has a look around and starts moving. Not away from me, but in a circle, sort of angling round me.

'Oh, bugger.' Tan'll sort it, he loves a bit of bother. So I whistle the dog. No dog. About now it is time to head casually to the fence, except there is a bull in the way. And no dog. Where the hell is the dog? Tan is never chained—there's no need up this no exit road—besides, he never wanders.

'Here Tan!' Edge towards the fence. Oh! Then my wife looks out the kitchen window. She walks out the back door to the fence, and I'm stuck in the middle of a paddock as a bull plays with me, and she wants to know what I'm doing.

'What's all the noise about?'

'Isn't it bloody obvious?' Christ, I didn't even bring a bit of wood with me. Then, faint barking a fair way off. 'Hey!' I can see things getting out of hand here.

'Go let Tan out of the pigsties!'

The next minutes are well stretched, and I'm pretty close to a pissed-off bull when Tan arrives—and, man, do I enjoy him snapping at that bull's heels for a bit, as they do the round-and-round-in-circles dance before the bull runs off in confusion. Some lessons are learned the hard way. I get off lightly, but from this day I'll never go into the bull paddock again without a solid stick. And I double-check to make sure my scavenging dog isn't in the pigsties drinking skim milk with the weaners when I head off home for breakfast after feeding them. He can stay with me from now on. And I know for sure I don't like, trust, enjoy or appreciate having bulls in my life. They've got a job to do and that's that. They are best on the other side of a well-constructed fence.

At some point after I contracted the viral meningitis that brought an end to my dairy-farming career, the nightmares started. By then I was living in Hokitika and working as a librarian, reading widely about all manner of things, getting lost in every book that caught my imagination and just occasionally wondering what I may have been missing.

When the phrase 'if you can remember the sixties, you must have missed them' was coined, I failed to see the joke. For me it seemed to be years of confronting the bull, both literally and metaphorically, and coming off second best all down the line. I wonder what I'd have thought if I knew there were twenty more years with the breath of a bull in my ears, and the pounding of my heart against my ribs, waking me night after night.

In 1980 I tried one more time to live a farming life. I got work as a shepherd at Titoki, inland from Whangarei. Six months later I was in hospital with unexplained back trouble, and that was that. Selling the horses and dogs, I had to move on; from the outdoors lifestyle, being my own boss, and having the pleasure of my own company. To put the issue another way, it was time to grow up. Ironically, the last day of active farming was bringing bulls across the big Lands and Survey block on horseback. The bulls got tired and grumpy, and more and more difficult to handle until, chasing one to head it off, my horse and I were airborne momentarily as a bull lifted us aside. Eventually the stroppy beast headed back to where he came from. And after that the nightmares started in earnest, often occurring for nights on end.

When the stock exchange suggests some action or other is bullish, the figure of speech is about an unattractive bovine characteristic. One thinks of pig-headed and bull-headed, or stubborn as an ox. Cattle and their behaviour inform our language out of the distant past. Who wants to be a silly old cow, or to roar like a bull while singing? Our language relates more readily to auroch, the wild bull, than to modern factory animals such as a herd of Friesian cows. The great beasts depicted in cave paintings throughout Spain and

France pay homage to auroch, the wild cattle that roamed European forests until late in the first millennium. With long curved horns and aggression to match, the beast stood over two metres at the shoulder and must have been utterly formidable. At least they are safely distant, securely tucked away in their limestone caverns or, maybe, books written by Romans or Greeks of the classical era.

We prefer to see the annual running of the bulls as a clip on television news or a photograph in the newspaper, rather than watch a dairy farmer putting cups on cows in a milking shed. Our culture prefers spectacle, and would rather pay attention to drama and danger, the charging bull of myth and screen. The twice-daily milking of three hundred or more dairy cows, which of course pays a large amount of the national trading account, is seldom seen as part of the same bovine evolution—it is far from spectacular in terms of audience appeal. We tend to prefer pets, and variety, so that even the daily chore of milking a house cow by hand is something most people would not look forward to. Once a season or two has provided context, however, the house cow becomes a different animal. There is her personality to consider, idiosyncrasies to make allowances for, and always the milk in the bucket to take back to the house.

Relax while you're told why I'm getting a new house cow. That is the first reason, to slow down. A little dun-coloured Jersey-Dexter cross cow will move through the next decade, and hopefully more, at a pace designed to suit her own nature. Try to rush or bustle her and we'll be in the shit—literally. I've got Taurus as an ascendant sign, and rushing isn't something that sets me up for the day either.

Regularly hand-milking the cow becomes a meditation of sorts—a second reason—getting up to wander out of the house before the others are awake. She'll be chewing her cud. Seeing me she'll get up, stretch, wander to the little yard then stand ready to be milked, still chewing her cud. Similar equanimity will greet all my voiced concerns: presidential elections, problems with women's minds, the insanity of authors, or how it's good to have family visit—and it's good to have them go again. Her large hairy ears will twitch with acknowledgement, and at the buzzing fly, while the great weight of her horned head will turn to gaze at my eloquence with genuine consideration as I bring the bucket and stool to her side.

Hand-milking is a knack, use it or lose it. That sound of squirting milk hitting the bottom of a metal bucket is evocative to any who may have milked a cow. Get it right and the cow (let's call her Heidi after my first house cow) will be patient; with maybe a belch or two for more cud to chew. Get it wrong and clean up the mess. Get it right and the habit is forged for a lifetime. She'll stand, you'll milk. Her ample flank will lean into your head and shoulder comfortably, you'll become part of the massive ribcage's breathing pattern for the few minutes it takes each day to strip her of milk. Get it wrong, and one morning for no known reason she'll lift a hind foot and place it into a bucket just about full of creamy milk. Of course mud or manure will cover her cloven hoof. Just when you need that cream later in the day. A chance switch round the ear from a sodden tail is something else worth keeping an eye out for.

Yet later in the day she'll wander over to the fence to have an ear scratched, to pick at some willow I've cut for her, or perhaps munch on winter hay. Or maybe she'll spend the night bellowing for a bull when she is in season. Heidi will be much more than just a milk factory. Maybe you should wander out one rainy winter day, just on dawn . . . sit beside a cow, steam rising off her flank . . .

At Gladstone we had our own cowman until recently, and old Ken found merit in the company of a couple of old raggedy cows, biking out from his old folks' home each day to cut some grass for his elderly charges. He was a returned

53

soldier, having served through the Second World War. Some of the soldiers who returned failed to settle back into society. They preferred their animals. Ken, who had been a tank driver in Italy, told me, 'Y'can trust a cow. She won't let you down.'

Another returned soldier was Alf Chinn, who actually managed to make the news in the *Hokitika Guardian* back in the 1970s with a story about the old Jersey house cow he'd milked every day for something like sixteen years, from the time she had first calved as a two-year-old heifer. During the Second World War, Alf had been a truck driver in the Supply Company, delivering goods to front-line troops. He received a mention in the battalion history for being lost for two days in the desert with his co-driver, when his unit had moved on during an action with the Germans. When I met him the war was twenty years past, and he used to come in to Hokitika library once a week and borrow two or three books, a small taciturn man who rolled his own cigarettes. Books in hand he'd head back out to Kaihinu where he lived, gardened, fished, and stayed out of trouble the best he knew how. There was no mention of his being wounded on Crete, or of the fighting in which he took part. It was from other sources I learned how Supply Company, plus transport units, cooks and other support troops, were part of the fierce defence of Galatos when the Allies were driven out of Crete. No one talked about the retreat over the mountains to beaches from which the fortunate were evacuated, the exhaustion and loss of friends in the fighting.

In the summer of 1964, while I was a student at Training College, I was sitting having a beer after haymaking with some farmers near Takaka. Two of them started talking. A sip of beer, a head bowed in concentration while rolling a cigarette.

'They crowded us on the decks,' one said. 'Then the stukas bombed hell out of us.'

'Did y'manage to get a feed?' the other asked. And so on, they talked. Quietly, without any fuss, they chatted in the warm twilight, excluding us from their experience. It was not the time for questions. They were just two men, elsewhere in their minds.

Alf had no wish to return to Crete, where bull jumping existed as a sport long before the kiwi became an emblem for our warrior nation's call to arms. New Zealanders on Crete were not there to wander among Minoan ruins, or gaze at pottery older than Christianity, on which depictions of bull jumping were painted. I wonder how many of them had any classical knowledge anyway. The cult of Mithra, with its ritual involving the cutting of bulls' throats and the drinking of blood, was the least of their concerns. Any ideas of how Mithraic custom merged into Christian practice had nothing to do with the lives of the average foot soldier on Crete in 1941. They were there to slow the advance of fascism, which they did alongside their allies, shooting German paratroopers out of the skies above Maleme airport (like so many ducks, Dan Davin told someone years later) and other sites where gliders swept in, unable to avoid their appointment with history and the rifles of well-trained Kiwis.

Nearly seventy years after the actions at Galatos and Maleme, New Zealanders travelling to Crete are welcomed as friends, I have heard. The actions of our fathers and grandfathers have entered the mythology of the place. As well as reading the war histories, I went in search of what was written about auroch, about bull jumping as an acrobatic display, and saw evidence of the way in which Crete and New Zealand met once at a moment in history, from which stories of great heroism could be told—and came away thinking about how soldiers act out the myths our countries live by. Carl Jung wrote about Nazi aggression, and the German nation living out the dark side of Teutonic mythology. It seems to me that any nation at war is in the process of rewriting the dark side of its mythological identity.

I did some rewriting of my own, and asked, 'What if Maui landed on Crete?'

Maybe his waka beaches one hot morning on some rocky foreshore, after he's been caught in the mother of all storms, blowing him a lifetime out of his way. This was a bad storm, obliterating all memory of the time before. So the trickster is here, knocked up a bit, coming ashore on the Cretan coastline, more dead than alive. Somehow he manages to stagger up the beach a bit, dying of thirst, exhausted, starved. He finds some shade provided by an ancient olive grove clustered round a spring trickling from rocks. Gradually he will drink. By and by his curiosity is sure to send him fossicking, lifting this stone, nudging at that fruit. Either that day, today, or some morning, he will arrive at the entrance to a cave, securely closed to outsiders. He will sneak a bit of a look, clamber over the mounded rock, checking things out. This is a being who has not heard of the Labyrinth, a being who isn't in the know, so to speak. Can you imagine Maui turning his back on such a cave? It is irresistible. No way is he going to just walk on and see what may be round the corner instead.

Winding the thong of his mere securely round his wrist, gripping that stout taiaha in his left hand, and knowing his footsteps can be sure and silent, he enters the deepening dark. This is no place for the fluttering piwakawaka or any other of his friends and helpers. Beneath the earth no sun burns down, to be held fast by the bravest of men who demands obedience. He moves beneath the earth right here, at the labyrinth entrance. Water drops from the rock above . . . drip drip drip . . . drip . . . hitting the floor to echo, or is it Maui's heartbeat echoing in his ears? So the path turns, following a twist in the cavern walls. Is this the last light that will reflect the glint in his wide brown eyes? What if the trickster of so many brave tales is to be lost forever beneath the crust of far away soil? Here is so far away from Moananui, where tidal currents are known, the flow of water and seaweed that tangles the paddle of the unwary. Underground there are no stars of the heavens, no Taki o Autahi indicating south, so surely guiding the prow of any waka home.

Could this Labyrinth capture the elusive Maui forever, under a land of harsh light, within black caverns where no chilly winter winds blow north from the snow and ice of Pou Tonga? Why, even pipiwharauroa, that great traveller, or kotiti haere the wanderer of the oceans with her great wingspan, have been left behind. Will no birds fly back with the gossip of this, his greatest journey? This is a warrior who is not short of bravery, though he has been known to be a little foolhardy at times. Today he will press on, lean from paddling through a great storm, tired from searching the heavens each night for familiar stars, blown by storm winds to this place. For what reason have the gods been so extravagant, Maui wonders?

After many twists and turns, with cuts and bruises on hands and legs from stumbling into rock, barely able to see, Maui arrives at a dimly lit place. Here, flickering torches burn, move shadows so that strange shapes jump at him, making him unable to be sure of his surroundings. Gradually, his eyes begin to see more. No birds fly so far underground, no fish swim out of the depths in this alien land of damp stones and darkness. But now he sees. In a far corner lurks a great beast. No! This is not a beast—rather it is half man, half beast. Maui's worst nightmares could not conjure up this monster.

Aroused by the scent of fear, the sound of shuffling human feet announcing an unexpected arrival, Minotaur raises his shaggy head, strikes at the dirt floor. Bellowing forth every ounce of air from his lungs, he fills the cavern with sound off the walls, a deep rumble of menace unlike anything heard before. With a shake of the great head, Minotaur lets light catch on the deadly horns sprouting from the bull's skull melded to the male body. Maui does not hesitate. The beast is answered with a cry. Raising his taiaha, he starts to haka. If this is death he will greet the stranger with courage and flair. Ka mate! Ka mate! His cry mingles with the bull's vast roar. Light stutters and flickers against horn and taiaha. Stamping feet, hoof against stone, raise dust, clouding movement. If Maui possessed a knife he might just slit this monster's throat to stop the noise. More sure of his footing and he'd somersault between those massive horns and drive the beast mad with his elusiveness. Between the eyes, a cleaving strike perhaps? Such a skull would surely be impervious to the most powerful clubbing of the strongest pounamu mere. Never has Maui seen such a creature on land.

Oh if only Tane was on hand to make a tree fall, trapping this strange man-beast beneath the stout arms of totara, or puriri. What if Tangaroa could bring one good wave to surge forth, swallowing up that mighty roaring in a gurgle of sand and kelp? As Minotaur moves that great bulk of his being more into the light, Maui sees the misshapen muscle, the vast strength of these misplaced genes, the result of such a vindictive union. He wonders at the games the gods play to sprout such an unlovely creature from a mythical queen's womb.

Then, when the very rocks of the earth seem to tremble, about to fall inward and bury them both, Maui understands what he must do. He remembers. His foot stamps down for the last time. Sweat streams from his glistening body, his chest heaves for breath to feed the heart pounding in his chest, and his hair drawn back and tied has fallen dishevelled across his broad back. A moment passes, and only paces away Minotaur pauses, confused. Bending slowly, ever so slowly, Maui never takes his gaze from the red-eyed stare of the beast. Gently, so as not to startle, Maui lowers his taiaha to the dirt. Next, he slips the mere thong from his wrist. In days to come, the gods will know Maui has visited this place. They will see he laid down his weapons in the presence of danger. Minotaur is not his to deal with. Maybe another being lives who will be part of this story. Rising to his full stature, Maui stands a moment, naked as warriors are, unarmed.

Now, he is gone. Like that, his presence is swallowed by shadow, as if he has never been here. Before the beast can move, Maui's footsteps can be heard in the labyrinthine darkness, fading away. We have no way of telling the beast, condemned as he is to live alone in darkness, deep in the labyrinth, that Maui must return to his waka. After finding his way home he has an appointment to keep, with Hine-Nui-Te-Po.

That was Crete. The New Zealand Expeditionary Force, like the Maui of my imagination, did not know what they were to face when they retreated from mainland Greece and her ancient gods to fight again on Crete. They once more faced the enemy bravely, before retreating. Many of them attracted the attention of Hine-Nui-Te-Po and found a home with her, so far from the night sky of the Southern Cross. Maui would have been proud if he had been there to watch the Maori Battalion charge, bayonets fixed, toward Maleme Airfield against all the odds. The heroism was not without cost.

Returned servicemen were different from those who had never 'gone away'. I sensed very strongly that Dad felt separated from other men of his generation because he didn't go overseas. He had his own problems of course, including the fact that he was rejected for service. For anyone, clothing may cover physical scars, but inside there are other beings that inhabit memory and imagination. Some of those who came home from war carried their memories, only to have their demons visit them in the night, when their guard was down. I am far from the only one to have dreams that waken me from sleeping in a state of terror. For many there is greater reason for their trauma to surface. In some respects given the history of our culture through the last two hundred years, it is a wonder most of us turn our lights off to sleep at all. There is so much lurking under the benign surfaces of our everyday actions, and the popular culture that is displayed in public.

I imagine the oldest hunger
infiltrating silhouetted dusk, see
that great bulk casting a darkness
as he mounts the dun heifer, then again
her scent of season, his lust. Urgent, the bull
goes hunting for more, a lick, questing
at the tail's base. The great shaggy head
being thrust skyward, lips curl as if he is
praising and mocking every ancient blood-
drinking god, in one foetid breath.

When you smell the rank body, it is
already too late. He is in the yard
among the herd. Already he is bellowing
summons a primeval challenge, a churning
of mud in bull paddocks up and down the valley.
He is breaching fences, breaking gates and bones
of dogs on his horns, head down he charges
across the page, to fuck your dream
to infiltrate your nightmare

Eventually most of us move on from events that knock our heads or bodies about. Time may not heal so much as soften memory's focus, blur some edges and remove intensity—but that is okay. Old soldiers stop crying out in their sleep, hearts begin to murmur, then go on to medication, and marching boots step slower, hesitate and falter. And happiness is always a possibility; when there is tender steak on the table ready to eat accompanied by a decent red wine, and someone to share it with.

We have meat from a yearling bull in the freezer, organic and home killed, from an animal that never threatened me. I learned at some point to side-step the black bull charging up the stairways of my dreams. There came a sense that maybe he was not going to get me after all, not quite, though he still called out and mocked, or roared his displeasure. The dream occurred less frequently. It appeared the bull was on vacation, or he had found some other soul to torment. Then one night the bull reappeared. The rack of horns was raised skyward and razor sharp, ready for whatever may come. There he was lying in a paddock, on the edge of my vision. While not quite chewing his cud, he was minding his own business, and more importantly, letting me mind mine.

Killing your own meat

Alec Wilson built his home at Purua during the Second World War. By milling a totara growing in his paddocks, he acquired sufficient timber to build the three-bedroom house that I rented off him during the winter of 1980. By then there was a beehive that had burst through the wall to occupy one room, while rats and opossums lived in the ceiling and walls. To occupy the building we had to clear the infestations with a .22 rifle, traps and poisons. Wheelbarrow-loads of dead bees were removed from what was to become a bedroom.

Alec was a generous and wise old man, steeped in local experience garnered from the pioneering of a hilly block of land that he turned from bush into a dairy farm. 'If you've got livestock, then you're going to have dead stock,' are the only words of his I can remember.

The words are vacuous, from the viewpoint of a society that obtains meat from a supermarket counter, and gets the local pest destruction officer to destroy wasp nests, vicious dogs and any other pesky creature that is out of control. For those who still live outside cities, and the numbers diminish with each year, it may not be quite so clear-cut.

I own a butchering knife, as do my farming friends. We own rifles.

'What are guns for?' my friend Mark asks his boys, who

are still attending the local primary school. They know the answer, but are shy in front of me. 'Killing things. That's the only thing they do. You don't play with them.'

And round here they are periodically used for their sole purpose—to kill a living creature. Thinking about this recently, and doing some tallying, it became apparent that killing has been a constant companion in my life.

I have killed for meat with a knife or rifle: deer, rabbits, from time to time a hare, sheep, pigs, young cockerels, old hens, on occasion a bull or steer, wild fowl, pukeko. All manner of fish I've caught with net, spear, bait or lure: eels, shark, kahawai, trout, and more besides, flounder, sole, gurnard, herring. Then there have been the maimed, ill or just plain pests that have been dealt to: gummy ewes, the cow with a broken leg, heifers and ewes at birthing, possums, wasps, magpies, dogs with a taste for blood, feral cats.

And then, when bush has been felled, or swamp drained, God alone knows what mayhem has been visited on the lives of the many small, crawling, swimming, flying creatures. About now I arrive at Gary Snyder's interpretation of the third Buddhist precept or teaching, which directs that we 'live doing the least possible harm'. It is not compulsory that we all, to paraphrase Roni Horn, set about remaking the place in which we live in 'the image of mankind'. Whether one is a farmer or a person on a city street, we have the same choice it seems: to live with awareness of the natural, of the animal self.

My widowed grandmother raised five sons while living on a block of a few acres, where she and the boys milked some cows and grew their own fruit and vegetables. She was, to quote a saying of my father's, 'tough as a goat's knee'. The boys, fatherless when the eldest was ten years old, put meat on the table from a variety of sources. An obvious and easy way was wringing the neck of surplus chooks or young cockerels. They could also be inventive, keeping a straight face as they greeted the local policeman, heading for home with poached trout stuffed down their trouser legs. There were fish for the taking offshore at Hampden near the Moeraki boulders in those days, and they would use handlines or nets to bring home flounder, cod, mullet or anything else they could catch. The trout, taken from streams rather than sea, were tickled as often as not.

As they grew older, the boys learned to shoot. I once saw my uncle, who worked as a shepherd, nonchalantly shoot a running rabbit with a .22 single-shot rifle. He just stood tracking the rabbit with the barrel, and by the time the report had finished echoing around the hills, the rabbit had stopped kicking on the other side of a gully. He had plenty of practice I guess, shepherding in Otago hill country where rabbits were an infestation of undesirable wildlife, eating pastures intended for sheep and driving farmers off their land.

Living in the country, shooting, and what went with it, was a fact of life. When I was a boy, firearms were easily seen and often accessible. Dad decided to clean his rifle while Stan Homer was sitting on the sofa chatting to him. When their ears stopped ringing, and Dad had recovered from the shock of firing a live round in the living room, they found the bullet hole. Neat as a new pin, through the window pane, it must have passed within a couple of inches of Stan's ear. I have done a similar thing myself, and put a bullet through the floor, after my 'empty' rifle was borrowed by someone. All we got through our lapses was a hell of a fright in each case. An incident like that only ever happens once. My father and I were fortunate.

One afternoon, when we lived at Maungaturoto, I watched from the kitchen window as a man hunted along the hillside, through scattered scrub growing on the farm next door to our house. He put up a cock pheasant and I watched the bird begin to tumble out of the air before the echo of the shotgun blast reached me. The bird fell heavily, struggled to rise a couple of times, then was still.

The hunting incident I remember best was also at Maungaturoto a little later. Dad took me out with a shotgun when I was twelve. He had borrowed the gun from a workmate, an old double-barrelled job with a slightly loose stock. His own single-shot gun was being repaired. We were hunting pheasant without a dog, which I learned later was like pie in the sky—and Dad knew it. Surprisingly, as we tracked through Yorkshire fog grass, knee high, and manuka scrub above head height, we did flush a fine cock bird. We'd walked past where he'd been concealed and camouflaged. He'd beaten us with stealth and didn't have to flush, but he did. I'd never heard a pheasant take off before, and the whirr of his wings gave me a hell of a fright. We turned and Dad swung up the gun, tracking the flight. Click! Nothing happened, except the bird gained height and disappeared beyond the canopy of manuka. I knew my Dad could swear, so it didn't bother me that he let rip about guns that misfired, hunting without a decent dog, bugger bugger bugger . . . and more.

Funny thing is, even though he had the bird dead to rights and plenty of time, he forgot to fire the second barrel. I'm grateful he didn't knock it out of the air. I've seen plenty of birds shot since then, but not many better sights than a mature cock pheasant rising against the angled afternoon sunlight of autumn, aglow with colour as he wound up against gravity and out of sight.

I never developed into much of a deer stalker. Up in the headwaters of the Taupiri River I went shooting with a friend from schooldays, and the first deer I ever shot lay dying. I had my knife out, ready to help her on the way. She looked up. The eyes clouded as I stood there, trying to decide what to do. Deer have huge soft brown eyes. Their browsing habits decimate the under-story of native forests if their population increases too much. Deer are considered vermin in this country, noxious pests. Yet, a doe and fawn in their natural habitat move with grace and harmony fit to inspire thoughts of beauty which may subvert the official view of them.

Since that occasion, other thoughts have come to mind. What could it do to the mind, making eye contact with another human that you have taken life from? Thank Christ I have never had to make a decision to shoot another human being. To a large extent my generation of New Zealanders has been spared that head-bending decision. My father-in-law once said to someone, not a member of the family, 'having to kill another man is a hard thing to do'. As he has since aged and died, there is no way of verifying his own experience of such things. Because he spent years overseas during the Second World War, firstly on active service, then later as an escaped prisoner of war on the run with partisan groups in the Italian mountains, it is possible he made that statement based on personal experience. We will never know. I suspect the statement was made in an unguarded moment, without his thinking his words would be picked up years later for interrogation.

As a young man I took part in military training during the Vietnam War years. We were never conscripted, and I am glad of that. At the time I would have gone if the government had sent us. As it happens the closest I got to conflict was scrubbing the barracks walls in the heat of several summer afternoons as a punishment for dusty boots, a minute speck of fluff up my rifle barrel or some other trivial offence. Perhaps I folded my blankets wrong on the bed.

Punishments could even affect a man's social life. One night down at the canteen, a couple of West Coast mates got a bit out of hand and nearly caused a confrontation with some humourless transport platoon trainees. Of course, I had nothing to do with the incident—I was too busy doing dress parades, another quirky, mindless punishment, which involved running from barracks to parade ground and back, changing into ludicrous uniform combinations to make us look ridiculous.

Army personnel were fond of a little light humour. When we were told to practise throwing pine cones to prepare us for a live hand-grenade exercise, I bowled a pretty good leg break across the throwing site. The sergeant, an immaculate Scot, was not amused. After a few accented expletives as he walked towards me, he stopped a metre away.

'We've got a punishment for the likes of you, laddie,' he roared. 'Masturbation with a glasspaper glove!' before storming off while the rest of the platoon giggled like a gaggle of fourth-form schoolboys.

Shortly after that episode we had an anti-tank grenade exercise. Attaching an armour-piercing projectile to our rifles, we attempted to demolish a car body fifty metres away. The grenades made a hell of a din, and holes in the ground all round the derelict vehicle showed we weren't great shots. During that exercise, my eardrums were ruptured and I lost my hearing completely. As we paraded, before our march back to camp from the practice range, I was unable to hear the orders yelled at our platoon. Consequently I did things wrong, or really late, which mucked up the drill. The NCO rushed over and started bellowing at me, turning just about purple in the process, but the louder he screamed in my face, the less I heard. All I got was a high-pitched distorted echoing in my head. Eventually he got the message. I was out of hearing, and out of action.

The army's fascination with giving recruits real experience of loud noises had left me with reverberations and not much else between my ears. Ten days of light duties saw me cleaning rifles and putting grease down their barrels so they could be stored away. Being unable to hear orders let me have me some peace and quiet for a time, but gradually the hearing returned—or some of it did, and I was out being yelled at again.

The war may not have been a good idea, but sending me would have been an even worse one, quite apart from my hearing which would have lasted no time at all. Vietnam seems to have been a hallucinatory experience—many drafted American and Australian soldiers, and the Kiwi forces who served in the combat zone, have suffered readjustment blues for decades since returning home. Being there would probably have dropped my mind in a morass of nightmares after five minutes, let alone a complete tour of duty. Just watching a film with graphic visual effects, such as Steven Spielberg's *Saving Private Ryan* or Coppola's *Apocalypse Now,* has had the power to give me a couple of months of recurrent bad dreams. Besides, the Buddha would say life is not ours to grant or take as casually as the rolling of a cigarette.

Eventually, killing animals for meat became distasteful, and moved me closer to a confrontation with something disturbing. To kill mutton, I would roll cigarettes and line them up on a rail in the yards, within easy reach. Throughout the process of cutting throats, skinning or gutting, I would ensure that a cigarette was smoking away between my lips. The smell of dead flesh was getting to me.

These days without the protection of the smell of burning tobacco I seldom kill at all. At times it is a necessary chore, but it is never one that leaves me undisturbed. Not so long ago, our dog Bess had to be put down. In times past I may have done the job, feeling it was my responsibility. This time at the vet clinic, I didn't administer the lethal injection, but held her still while she looked up at me for reassurance—and the intensity faded from her eyes.

I still have the old single-shot .22 rifle hung out of sight, obediently chained and secured as regulations demand these days. The .44 Winchester carbine, similar to that used by the US Cavalry in a thousand Westerns—the sort where countless 'red Indians' fall off their galloping horses to die, as the soldiers fire from bottomless magazines—I sold while living in Northland. It was owned by various members of the family over two or three generations, and used for pig shooting or deer stalking in heavy bush country. It got sold because I was short of cash, and because I didn't go shooting any more.

Late one afternoon last summer I walked along the bank of the Ruamahanga with my fishing rod. The afternoon was hot, and alive with the buzz and hum of insects soaking up the heat and, like the cicada clinging to the grey-barked willow, getting on with their noisy business. Leaves on the willow looked tired and ready to drop even though their green had not yet turned to yellow or brown. Having arrived in the shade, it seemed a good idea to sit for a while, right where the grassy bank looked over a deep pool formed by a tangle of roots and windfall tree trunks. As I settled down, getting used to the movement of light through the water below me, a trout flicked lazily into view. That certainly got me looking more closely. Dropping out of the branches forming the wide dappled canopy above me were willow bugs. These tiny creatures caused dark red calluses in most of the leaves above me, and they were now releasing themselves from the willow and dropping in their hundreds to the river below. In my tackle bag I had flies tied to simulate this hatch, tiny feathered objects with a yellow bead as a head, designed for use at precisely this time of year.

Another trout turned lazily to rise and pluck a fallen bug out of the current just below the surface. Moments later a third showed its pale belly as it rolled gently to take a bug. As I watched, the first trout came back from the darker side of the pool to suck another mouthful. These good-sized fish were feasting with a casual approach to the whole business, as if there was all the time in the world. Gently they circled the hole, allowing the bugs to fall and swirl on the current as it washed back and round, seeking a release into the main channel of the stream. Sunshine filtered through the water to shine on the bodies of the fish, lighting the freckled brown dots on their scales momentarily, flickering over the movement of a fin, or thrust of a powerful tail. From where I was, I could watch the fish feed unaware of my presence. In a pool so filled with snags and willow roots, it was pointless to get my rod and line into play. I just sat there watching.

While we were carrying out exercises in the foothills of the Southern Alps, during army training forty years ago, two or three of us got separated from our platoon. We were by a stream that looked likely for trout, with its shingle bottom, clear water and high banks. Sure enough I did see a trout, browsing beside an old tree trunk which was half in, half out of the water. Lying along the log as quietly as possible, I placed my hand in the water, loose and relaxed, a little behind the fish. Christ that water was cold. Slowly, I edged my fingers forward, until I felt the belly of the fish. Gently now, take your time, I talked my hand forward gently stroking the belly of the fish . . . closer to the gills . . . closer. I turned thumb and forefinger to be either side of the body moving with the water—

But, on this bank, I had no urge to hunt these speckled fellows that fed on the hatching willow bug. Here I was audience to a ritual dance, a ballet of grace, power and sustained beauty. The music of the natural world provided the score if one wanted to listen. Late summer was a lazy choreographer, and the laying on of fat to help trout survive the winter, a prosaic storyline. There would be another day to cast my line, to create mayhem hooking a fish in some other pool. Leaving the bank as quietly as I had arrived, the slant of the sun told me it was time to go home. Catherine would be expecting me for dinner.

There was a deeper reason to be wary of weapons, a reason

that I didn't care to admit most of my adult life—a memory of grownups' manipulative games overflowing with malice and threat. Of my father sitting in the living room with no lights on, cleaning and oiling his rifle for a couple of hours on end after an argument with Mum. It happened more than a time or two—just as more than once my mother told me during my teenage years, 'Go and hide the gun before your father gets home.' If Dad was late arriving home from work and staff from head office had arrived in town, she knew he was likely to be away 'having a few' with them at the pub. Mum disliked beer and whisky, and intensely disliked weapons. She would not contain her irritation with his late arrival, often playing 'no speaks', such a childish, yet with Dad's background, deadly and provocative response. And when my father sat in that room with a gun lying across his knees, us boys knew to draw absolutely no attention to ourselves as we crept round the house.

I have inherited my father's diaries. From that time, round 1960, aside from brief entries about trout fishing and gardening—or the weather perhaps—are the telling words 'had a few'.

Who are the
Don Cossack Choir?

With the appetite of someone who's had plenty to drink and
little to eat, night after night Dad took over the kitchen.
There'd be the coal range to stoke up, then white bread to get
out of the cupboard, with butter and cheese from the fridge.
Slice after slice of bread, with lashings of butter, reinforced
with wedges of cheese, would be eaten. Cigarette smoke
would hang in the air, and cups of tea used to wash down
the bread and cheese. My father would be centre-stage telling
his yarns that, often as not, I'd heard before. From time to
time one or other of my brothers would walk in and help out
with demolishing the bread and cheese. Even after she came
home, Mum would be in bed, recovering from her months in
hospital with tuberculosis.

'That man,' Dad would shake his head in disbelief,
'that a man could sing like that, when he was dying from
tuberculosis!' We did not have to be told he was thinking
about the Don Cossack Choir member he watched singing
the solo in 'Monotonously Rings the Little Bell', a searing
melancholic piece of Russian folk music.

In 1926 my father heard the Don Cossack Choir perform
in Christchurch.

He was eighteen years old and remembered their singing
for the rest of his life.

Their records were among the first purchases to be played on the stereo that was bought in Rotorua during 1958. We quickly became familiar with the mix of bravado, exuberance and extreme yearning expressed through their singing.

Historically the Don River Cossacks were mercenaries for the tsar, as well as bandits or brigands from time to time. As a result of the Russian Revolution and the victory of the Red Army, by 1919 or 1920, large groups of Cossacks found themselves refugees in Turkey. It was here that Serge Jaroff, a young lieutenant who had received musical training in Moscow, decided to get some of his men singing to raise morale. His group of *a capella* choristers developed a repertoire of Russian folksongs and religious music, and sang their hearts out. In exile they sang songs of home, in the best tradition of all the songsters who long to be back where they belong but are no longer able to dwell.

The story from there is like the plot of a novel. Their growing fame transported them via Europe to the United States. Performance took them everywhere around the world, except back to their homeland Russia.

In 1926 Dame Nellie Melba invited the Don Cossacks to sing in Australia, and it seems logical that they would have visited New Zealand on that trip. Dad did hear them perform and he never forgot their singing. Every so often he would tell again his memories of the concert, as often as not when alcohol had loosened his tongue. He could proclaim at length—most often, it seems now, when I was sitting at the kitchen table trying to do homework or swot for exams during my fifth and sixth form years at Grey High School. In other words, when I needed to be doing something other than listen to him.

I just can't imagine my saying, 'Hey Dad, I'm busy swotting just now', back then.

Dad was sent out to do gardening with his younger brother Alan each week during class singing. He would tell us kids that as a joke, but I'm not sure it ever was. Every so often he would croak out a line or two in a drab monotone—'I look for zee angel, but zee angel are so few', or 'gone are ze days, when my heart vas young and gay'—and then wander off to the garden chuckling to himself. Things were always good when he felt like chanting,

I had a little dog and his name was Ben,
he had nine tails and jolly near ten . . .
and he chased them round the room
. . . with a broom.

In my book, to be allowed to sing, regardless of quality, is a basic human right. People who feel they are superior about singing in tune or in time around the house disgust me. Many a squabble would start during the dishes. We'd be singing, then someone would pipe up, 'That's not the right words.'

'It is so!'

'Hey Mum,' and there would be instant escalation. Besides, who could choose which song to sing? 'Sara Sue I'm sad and lone—'

'Hey I was singing!'

'You were not—'

'Was so!'

'Evening shadows leave me blue, when—'

'I told you. You don't know the words.'

Next thing there were tears, someone flounced out—and it was all over words in a bloody song no one knew the words of for sure. And that's me, sounding just like my father after a few drinks. I never remembered the words, and in the end trying to sing at the sink was not worth the fuss and bother. Anyway, Dad was told he couldn't sing, yet he admired the singing of some performers with passion. The Don Cossacks and Joseph Schmidt were heroes, and perhaps

Paul Robeson, one of the great bass voices of the twentieth century. What they had in common was voice quality, and a history of persecution in their lives. And Dad saw their singing as politically subversive for one reason or another.

Joseph Schmidt was born a Rumanian Jew in 1904. Because he was only just over 150 cm in height, he was denied the chance to become an opera singer of note. A great lyric tenor, his voice perfectly suited the new medium of radio as broadcasting developed during the 1920s and 1930s. He trained in Berlin, and gained international fame for his concert performances. Later on, his fame grew as he starred in a number of film musicals.

My father would have become familiar with his voice through radio more likely than film. After the record player appeared in our home, there was always a Joseph Schmidt record to listen to. The 45 rpm 'extended play' disc featured 'A Star Fell from Heaven' plus three other songs, possibly including 'Tiritomba', which I learned in standard three or four at Welbourne Primary School, New Plymouth.

After establishing his career and international fame during the 1930s in spite of the rise of fascism, Schmidt spent the war years trying to find a safe haven in Europe. I can remember my father telling me Schmidt was put in Auschwitz where he died. After a few drinks at the pub, during my teenage years, Dad would arrive home thoroughly stirred up. 'How could they put a voice like that in a gas oven?' he'd say with anguish in his voice, overcome with the enormity of it all. My father's exclamation 'How could they put a voice like that in a gas oven?' on those late evenings was as much about my father as about Schmidt. For me, the pain of his exclamation carries an emotional punch to this day. Yet, the funny thing is, my father didn't know the facts.

In 1942 Schmidt was interned in a Swiss refugee camp, although he was well known and possessed an American visa. In November of that year he died from disease and exhaustion. In 1960 we didn't own computers to Google the facts of any biography we chose. Joseph Schmidt with the amazing lyrical tenor voice was not gassed by a Nazi in a concentration camp. Effectively his life was terminated by a petty Swiss bureaucrat who was afraid to do anything that might offend the Nazi regime. An anonymous rubber stamp allowing him passage to the United States was refused Schmidt the Jew. Although the principle was spot on, Dad got the details wrong.

In the paradoxical world of his day-to-day existence, Dad would seldom have actually listened to those voices singing while I was growing up. Most often the radio was commandeered by older brothers or sisters, listening to hit parades or 'The Goon Show', or 'Life with Dexter'. Anyway, Dad became more and more deaf as the years went by, physically and quite possibly socially. I wonder if the clamour was more than he could be bothered with. Often enough, he'd sit silently in company, having turned off the hearing aids he wore from his fifties till his death at ninety.

I sympathise with the deafness. My own world changed radically when, close to sixty, I got hearing aids. Now I also joke about being able to wake in a quiet world, and having to use technology if I even want to hear a bird sing. Music I thought I knew on record or compact disc had whole sections of violin, or similarly high-pitched instruments playing notes that I had no idea existed. Something like the beginning of *Lark Ascending* by Ralph Vaughan Williams was beautiful music for decades—but I didn't know how beautiful. Only with hearing aids am I able to hear the first few delicate bars of solo violin or the final section. Listening to the human voice has its fair share of problems as well, so it is no surprise that Dad just gave up trying. So many people mumble, speak without facing the person they're talking to, or in some other way speak indistinctly, like calling out from the next room, or the other side of a closed door. It can be difficult enough to hear clearly anyway, even with the aids stuck in your ears like corks, as if to keep your brains from falling out.

Not long ago I came across a record, *The Best of the Don Cossack Choir*, absolutely by chance. There it was, tucked in an unlikely carton of records from which we were invited to take any we desired. This scrap of vinyl, a twelve-inch LP, had belonged to the recently deceased father of a friend. In mint condition, it appeared to have never been played right through. I couldn't wait to get home with my find. We'd recently bought a record turntable to play the old records from the sixties and seventies we still have stashed away in cartons. Listening, I wasn't quite prepared for what took place—the power of these voices, their ability to communicate emotion.

My old man, his late-night harangue sessions, his help-lessness in the face of anguish, his anger at injustice, the remembered sound of his voice welled up, echoing in the room with the singing from the Don Cossack Choir. Dad is ten years dead. I am unable to let him know how moved I was to hear this singing again. Perhaps the voices evoke what music could do for Dad.

Back in 1926, he was a country boy working in the city as a railway cadet. When confronted by those Cossack voices singing with palpable longing for what has been lost, listening to the songs coming from that stage in Christchurch, something had been stirred in Dad. Two dozen exiled Russians dressed in drab black uniforms sang for something they could never farewell: their families and childhoods, their livelihoods, and most of all, their homeland Mother Russia and the black soil of the land through which the Don River swept. One young man in their audience recognised something. Jack White, by eighteen years of age, had seen enough of life to know loss and longing when he heard it.

Heroes

Nineteen fifty-six. I saw the Springboks beat Northland in the mud at Whangarei. At the same ground on a sunny summer afternoon that year I saw the West Indian cricketers beat Northern Districts. What about the All Blacks who beat those same Springboks in a four-match series, or the Kiwi cricketers who won their first-ever victory against any side in a test against the West Indians at Eden Park? Those sportsmen were all heroes to twelve-year-old boys like me.

We shifted to Maungaturoto just after school started that year. For Mum it couldn't have been more inhospitable, a small farming settlement ninety miles north of Auckland. We moved into the usual three-bedroomed house on railway row: Mum, Dad and kids—four boys and, by then, only one older sister still at home. The other two came home every so often for visits. Half a dozen weatherboard state houses, all painted the same creamy yellow outside, lined up along a shingle track rising away from the station where Dad was the new stationmaster. To get to school, shops or the church was a five kilometre trip along a narrow unsealed road that wound past rolling hills, between rough half-developed farms, or through cuttings overgrown by gorse and blackberry.

The first morning at Maungaturoto District High School set the tone for the lives of my younger brothers and me. Chris was in standard three, Keith in standard one, I was older and in standard five. They came looking for me at morning playtime, arriving in time to stand close as a circle of barefoot, shirt-tailed, dirty-kneed boys gathered.

Only one of them spoke.

'So you're the new pricks are yuh?'

In my memory, it seemed a while before Chris and Keith spent any time outside class without seeking me out. At one stage Chris's lunch was regularly being stolen. Even with Mum belting him all the way down to the school bus stop beside the station, he'd rather throw tantrums than go back to that place. I'm not sure it was much better at home. Keith took to chewing his finger nails till they bled. When one of my sisters got pissed off with my older brother, the fork she threw across the table at him stuck in the wall inches from his head. The same wall he put his fist through in frustrated rage another time. That wall and I had rice thrown over us more than once, when Dad's short fuse got the better of him while trying to make me eat the claggy, unpalatable, over-boiled stuff.

'Maunga-ta-bloody-roto' became Mum's phrase of choice whenever anything got out of hand. She gave up gardening when the fork tines bent backward in the rock-hard pipe-clay soil outside our back door.

Meanwhile, at school, our teacher told us we were going to start writing with pens and ink. The girls got first go, which was fair enough. Theirs are always the neatest books. With their hands holding the dip pen just so, between thumb and forefinger, and their exercise books at just the right angle to get slope . . . oh wow.

This was grown-up stuff. Eventually my turn came. I'd never noticed there was a difference between right and lefthanders before. Of course I used a knife and fork cack-handed but who cared, the food still found my mouth. Writing was not like eating.

Our teacher, a round-faced, chubby-cheeked, curly-haired

hit with the girls, was a fanatic about writing—the right way. Molly Timpson with the wavy blonde hair could call out 'Albert' at lunchtime and he might laugh—but when it came to writing, lefthanders like me were stuffed. You had to hold the pen right and put the book correctly on your desk, or you'd be in trouble with a ruler across your knuckles, and before long a strapping. I'll defy anyone to write left-handed according to the manual for 1950s instruction and not smudge their work. One morning my name appeared on the blackboard along with a couple of others. We were dorks to be sneered at, to be the butt of jokes, having not grown up yet. Back to pencils for us.

Exam time arrived. For some reason we suddenly had to use ink again. In arithmetic I got almost everything right. Ink smudges though? That was another thing entirely. Next day that teacher, he was fair bristling, slamming our exam papers down on our desks as he handed them back.

'Out the front you!' he snarled at Alistair McDonald. Then Philip Collinson and, I think, Tony Linton.

'Hold your hand out.' Alistair got four of the best. Then Tony. Tears spilled, as hands held tightly under armpits still burned. My turn.

I put my hand out.

'Higher!'

'I said higher!' My hand went up to shoulder height, where my arm couldn't give when the hit came. The thick leather strap arced over his shoulder. CRACK!

I was not going to cry.

'Other hand!' Four of the best. A long way back to my desk. 'Don't look at anyone.' I'd learned to recite that to myself from somewhere. Just like I learned at home to never make a fuss. Dad would always turn to where the noise was coming from.

That man's attempted smile after the act of strapping lives with me, but no memory of the rest of the morning in class

80

remains. What I do remember is us boys milling round at lunchtime.

'You should go to Mister Wyatt,' someone said.

'They can't strap us for exams,' was another opinion. For me the headmaster was not an option. Wyatt had the sympathy of a bull in a paddock.

My wrists were beginning to swell. Red welts across the other boys' hands looked hot and sore. Mine were unmarked, but round my wrists were bruises and broken skin where the leather had wrapped and torn. To this day I don't know how that man lost his aim four times in a row. There was a lot of talk, until the bell went. Everyone just turned, drifting off to class. I started walking. Out of the playground, down the street, past the houses, beyond the footpath and the asphalt. I was heading home . . . no gathering of bags, telling nobody. It was hot and dusty, and when the town faded from view round the corner, I half-trotted, half-walked. By now I was crying. Every time I heard a car, it was over the bank to hide in the gorse and blackberries. Silence. I'd clamber back onto the road, and dogtrot some more. Over five kilometres without being caught. Dad wasn't at the station, so I walked on past it and headed for home, looking for Mum.

Dad went after my teacher later that afternoon, wanting to draw some blood himself. Mum bandaged my wrists. For days my hands were painful to use. I never went back to that school. A couple of weeks later the school year ended, and in January we moved to Rotorua. My Dad had gained a railway promotion, and I started having nightmares.

In one of those 'small country, you know who' moments, my sister heard this story from Alistair McDonald not so long ago, close to fifty years after it happened.

'He never cried. He ran away from school. Pat was our hero.'

Why didn't I see myself as a hero in that incident? Over the past fifty years of telling that story, how come I was never the hero but always the victim? For years I played a lot of sport. Sometimes I probably even played well from time to time.

'Do you know much about the sport I played?' I asked my son Andrew a few days ago.

'Yes,' he said. 'You started to get concussion when you played rugby, so you gave it up.'

'Anything else?'

'Did you play much else?'

One thing I've not indulged in is telling my sons about any of it. Maybe it would have helped them to have heard a bit more.

If we wanted to play at secondary school level, Mum insisted that any washing be done by us. Money for gear was not available. And practices were not to interfere with things like being home to do the grocery shopping or other chores. All of which was fine. I made sure she had little cause for complaint, and made it into school teams anyway—I loved sport for goodness' sake.

'You're not playing rugby,' she insisted in my School Certificate year. 'You needn't think we're paying for you to go to school an extra year, just to hurt yourself playing sport.'

'But Mum . . .'—protest, as always, was pointless. So I'd played goalie in the school hockey side, where players such as future national rep Bill Thomson used me for target practice when his Christchurch West High School side thrashed our inept team by a score so high they lost count. Now that was scarily dangerous, but Mum had her way. She didn't like rugby.

If I featured in interschool games of cricket and got my name in the paper, which happened sometimes, it was Dad's turn. The time I took three catches in an innings and got an honourable mention was his chance to talk about the catch he took for the Railwaymen's Social Club in God Knows Where, one afternoon in the 1920s. If I happened by some fluke to score a try at rugby it would remind him of the one he saw Jack Steel score in 1926—or whatever. I don't remember Dad ever watching me play a game of cricket, rugby or hockey, or tiddlywinks for that matter. Seems I was never going to be good enough to get the credit. Thinking about it from this distance, it seems a mixture both laughable and sad. As a boy I longed for once—just once—to be good enough for my father to accept that, and not to tell his own story. When I answered questions about how a game went, somehow everything turned to shades of grey.

I suppose we have to become our own heroes in the end, but how does that happen? Being not quite athletic, not quite academic in a house full of bright bastards didn't help me find a way.

John invariably would say 'I know' if I offered information.

'It's going to rain.'

'I know.'

'What is the word for—?'

'Don't you know?' would be the sneered response.

In the end I became the expert of laid back, nothing fazes me. And found trivial acts of subversion a source of comfort. My brainy mother and father used to leave books of crossword puzzles in the dunny, and there they'd sit for long periods of time, pen in hand, puzzling away. As they grew up, my brothers and sisters joined in this game, and they'd skive off to perch, doing a crossword—especially during prime time when dishes were to be done, or wood collected or other chores like washing to be brought in off the line.

That I couldn't get the hang of crosswords was cause for smirks, and more 'I know' stuff. My resentment festered and grew. I got a couple of those books, and wrote random but totally irrelevant words, that nonetheless fitted appropriate spaces, for page after page. Understandably, one or two people didn't see the humour of that effort. Cross words were spoken. I felt better though. Even as kids, in our own small, mismatched, mucked up world, sometimes there was a chance to fight back.

Longing

I look out in the darkness. Well after midnight, a full moon shines through the bedroom window of my concrete-block flat. Weird half-lit shadows flit across bookcases and walls. It may be the booze, being stoned or just the unlikely wisdom of utter weariness, but suddenly I am fed up with the shapes quivering and moving over the great pale sphere. I've had enough of the unstated threats crowding my mind, while features of my mother's face take shape in the shadows. I am done with weeks of crying, and only a few days into my decision to keep on trying in spite of whatever is haunting me.

'It's over,' I tell the moon, my mother. 'You can't get me now.' Rolling over, I sleep, to wake the next morning feeling like a different person, still so fragile, but somehow stronger.

I wish I could say that once I left home the wandering ways of my father were left behind, but for over twenty years I continued to shift, at times even more obsessively than he had. There was no grudge match with a number of faceless names on a railways staff list for me. Instead, I was simply longing. What for?

I thought it was a particular sort of place, a definitive town, or a special site, perhaps a unique outlook or a soul mate. Even a stable identity of some sort might have helped,

I suppose. Recently I read Richard Nelson's *The Island Within* and had a moment of recognition when he wrote: 'As time went by, I also realized that the particular place I'd chosen was less important than the fact I'd chosen a place and focused my life around it.' But that insight lay far into the future when I first struck out on my own. The idea that physical belonging meant getting to know somewhere, and it didn't matter where, was beyond me through the wandering years. When I leased the farm at Blackwater, I had plans to be there for as long as I breathed. After two seasons and a dose of leptospirosis, a type of viral meningitis, I left there with my wife and a toddler son, and a debt to pay back for failing to fulfil the four-year leasehold contract.

A house on the beach at Hokitika was good therapy, and I was happy there. Then we moved on, to the delight of everyone but me. No one else can be blamed. It was my action in applying for another job that made the shift necessary. By getting a bigger job in Ashburton, I was showing my potential. I was also trying to please my wife.

'That's great news,' Dad had said when I told him we were shifting. When I told him the salary I would be on, he replied, 'I'm proud of you m'boy. That's a good screw.'

Being on a good screw was important to Dad. While income may have been important to him, being on a good screw just about screwed me up. Ashburton was also where I first spent time incapacitated with back pain. From there, where I occupied four houses in four years and my marriage ended, I moved to Dunedin. A bigger job (with an excellent screw) beckoned me south, and there were four shifts of house within two years and a new partner. During that time I bought a block at Moeraki. It was leasehold land where a grove of kowhai trees cast dappled shade over pasture. Above the township it had expansive views, south down the coast toward Shag Point, and north over the Moeraki boulders to Hampden where Dad grew up. I slept in a tent one night on that block before moving to Northland. With no point in owning land so far away, it was then sold. In Northland, the same pattern continued. Absolutely stopped in my tracks with back problems, we shifted five times in less than four years. By then I was chasing the dark side so hard it was no longer possible to see much light. To hide from myself required more and more activity, more and more movement.

By the time I 'celebrated' forty, however, the running was over. If I ever wanted to have any peace of mind, or bodily health, it was clear even to me that I had to find some other way of living. A year earlier I'd flushed my own personal pharmacy of painkillers down the toilet: Brufen, Indocid, SRA—slow release aspirin, Melleril.

'Why did they prescribe that?' my nursing sister Beryl asked. 'Melleril is only used by terminal patients with real pain problems.'

'How would I know?' I likely replied. 'Ask the doctor.'

I could have said the pain in my back was the least of my problems. Prescription drugs did nothing for the state I was in. Painkillers cushion pain—so more injury could be inflicted on my damaged spinal discs because I just kept on with patterns of self-harm. Without the pills to medicate my back, I took to home-brewed wine and dope. A couple of tumblers of pear wine could end all pain for the rest of the day. Yet, sure enough, the next morning, the problems arrived back, about the same time as consciousness. Why should I be surprised that the solution did not really do a great deal to help? My back still hurt—but at least I knew it was hurting. The mental fog resulting from taking painkillers, anti-inflammatories and whatever else had been prescribed over the years by doctors, was lifting. An indication of how fuzzy things became can be taken from a two-metre high corrugated iron fence thirty metres long that I built in Northland. When I saw it again, a while after leaving, I had no memory of that building activity taking place. It must have been a major undertaking but my head was elsewhere at the time. That is how it was for a few months, while a different pain was waiting to have its turn.

Depression that had lurked beneath the surface for years produced an unravelling: of my second marriage, of life with my own children and stepchildren, along with almost any sense of personal identity that had managed to survive the decades of punishment I'd dealt out to myself. Without work, women or kids, and nobody on whom to project reasons for the way things turned out, I was exposed. My resources seemed pitifully inadequate. Two marital separations, and the resulting property settlements, left little in the way of material goods to weigh me down. What I was doing was moving, as surely as walking a concrete pathway, toward obliteration of the self. Each time there was a glimpse of happiness, it would be scuttled. There was always a good reason. That was part of the game being played out, at others' expense. I had a deep mistrust of good things that came my way, and while striving to seek out those positive situations, somehow I had to move on from them before suffering some sort of hurt that had no name. Facing up to the destructiveness of that way of living was painful enough eventually to push me over the edge into the depression that had been waiting for me over years. That, of course, is hindsight, gathered while trying to pick up the pieces. At that time in Northland I was the last to see sense in anything, while living on the very knife-edge I'd been very good at recognising when I saw it in others. Now it was my turn to choke on some humble pie.

My rescue, if that is what took place, occurred through meeting some people who accepted me without judging. But there were one or two false starts, like my visit to a hypnotherapist. In three regression sessions, I let the therapist lead me back into my childhood. He had me questioning all manner of incidents from the past.

At one point under hypnosis, I was smelling fear, from Dad's hands. During the 1940s while living in Southland, there were times when he spent every weekend shooting rabbits, for meat and for money from their pelts. A consequence of the constant handling of hides and carcases is that the smell of dead meat and something feral seeps into the skin of a person.

In the final session, by asking the right questions, the hypnotist took me further back.

'My mother looked at me when I was born, then turned away. She didn't want another boy.' In response to another question I continued, 'Somebody else in the room wrapped me in a grey woollen blanket. It was rough on my skin.'

That was the end of the therapy. There was no knowing what the facts were from that far back. I did know how I felt about it though, chewed up and spat out. The treatment was money down the drain. Visiting formative experiences during therapy is fine, but the follow-up to that sort of exposure is as important as the opening up. After hypnotherapy I was left to fend for myself.

Since then I have been interested in what happened in my family during my early childhood. For whatever reason, I had felt a misfit much of the time. Comparatively recently the term 'replacement child syndrome' has come to my attention. I read about the term in Martin Edmond's book, *The Resurrection of Philip Clairmont*. Apparently Clairmont was a fair example of the syndrome. So, I discovered, was Vincent Van Gogh, when I read about him seeing his name on a gravestone to which he was frequently taken by his mother. He had a younger brother who died as an infant, who had been the first recipient of his given names.

One of the difficulties that a replacement child has is they can never live up to the ideal, and forever unfulfilled, image of one who goes before them. Another problem for them is, because they are always travelling in the shadow of the other being, they struggle to find their own identity. The syndrome can occur if parental grief gets subverted, or stuck in some way, when a child dies.

Mine was a homebirth, in a railway house away from the main settlement of Tapanui. Was I born in the same room as that in which my mother had a stillborn daughter two years earlier?

I decided recently to ask my sisters if they could shed any light on this elusive family story and phoned each of them. Lesley has no idea at what stage of the pregnancy the dead baby left Mum's body. Elena says she feels it was at about six-and-a-half months. Beryl is the youngest of my sisters and has no recollection of my mother ever talking to her about it at all. I spoke on the phone to my sister Elena.

'Mum told me,' she says, 'that she felt unwell and went to the toilet. Then, her waters broke and the baby arrived.'

'She called it a baby?'

'Yes,' she goes on. 'But it was already dead.'

'So it was stillborn?'

'Well, she may have said it breathed a couple of times, but died more or less straight away.'

Then it was my oldest sister Lesley that I phoned.

'I don't know,' she said. 'I think Keith's wife, Cathy, told me that Mum said to her, it came in the bath.'

'But Mum didn't say anything to you?'

'No. Not that I recall.'

My parents lived in Tapanui during most of the Second World War years. In 1942, a year that saw my sister Beryl fall sick with pneumonia three times, and during which my father had three months off work for stress-related sick leave, my mother became pregnant. After Lesley and Elena were born, she had been told that it would endanger her health to be pregnant again. Alone at home, with four children still under six years of age to look after, my mother's pregnancy ended spontaneously.

What all of us kids do know is that Mum always said she had eight children. Seven were alive, and one was not. In a sense we knew everything and nothing at the same time. My sisters, who then were all very young, do not remember any fuss or bother, nor any funeral or burial. Lesley told me that she and Elena stayed with someone at Tapanui, while Mum took Beryl and John to Hampden and stayed with Gran White, Dad's mother, for a while. Among the ghosts of the past, I seem to recall someone saying Mum buried the baby in the garden. I told my sisters, seeking some sort of corroboration of the story. It would have been a terrible thing for my mother to live through.

'I've no idea where that one came from,' one replied.

'It's possible,' another said. 'Mum never seemed to look pregnant when she had you younger lot. Maybe she and Dad were the only ones that knew?' Another question without an answer.

'In those days women didn't always go to the hospital if they had pregnancy trouble. I've searched all the genealogical records, and no stillborn Patricia was recorded with the right details about that time.'

Mum said more than once, the baby was a perfectly formed little girl. Two of my sisters mentioned that point. She called her Patricia. Decades later, something that upset her when Beryl's baby died was the naming. That little girl was named Susan Patricia. As Beryl pointed out to me on the phone today, coincidence was involved. Her husband had a sister named Patricia who died when she was forty, and Susan was named in honour of Beryl's sister-in-law, rather than a sister she never knew.

Lesley told me one last thing when we talked yesterday, and it was no real surprise.

'When she got so bad with emphysema, Mum said to me not to let them resuscitate her. She wanted to be with those two little babies, Patricia and Susan Patricia.'

From 1942 Mum lived with a grief she was unable to let go. Two years later, in 1944, in the same house Patricia had died in, I was born and named Patrick.

'We went to school in the morning,' Elena told me. 'And you were there when we got home in the afternoon.'

I do not know enough about psychology to do more than ask questions. The question this time being—why I was given the male version of a name used for a baby girl who was born dead? And another question occurs to me. Did I remind Mum of what she had lost every time she looked at me? The process of grief and loss is mysterious, and while men may feel loss of a stillborn, they are not the ones who have invested their bodies and heartbeat in the provision of life for that body within a body.

Fortunately for me, others, without the benefit of hypnotherapy, were prepared to be more nurturing. Although I was spending time writing and painting, those activities tied me to the flat and there were times when I had to get out from the confining walls, into sunlight. I'd have done anything to stop the voices of mockery and failure having their conversations inside my head. Because the flat I had rented was quite central, walking up town for a coffee, or some meaningless errand, was an easily available way to distract myself. Too much time on my own was just a bit hard to take. A new pizza café had opened quite handy. There, in what became an almost daily moment of warmth and welcome, John and Nick would give me a free coffee in return for a bit of help preparing some of the toppings, or sometimes they'd even offer a pizza before I went on my way.

I bought a bike on lay-by, and after three weeks of payments the shop owner called me out the back.

'You'd better take the bike with you,' he said.

'But what about the payments?' I managed to get out.

'You'll pay,' he said. 'The bike's not doing either of us any good sitting out the back.' Once again I was glad of the dark glasses I had taken to wearing. Every time some kind thing happened I couldn't keep back the tears. Buying that bike, which took the place of a car for financial reasons, turned out to be one of the best decisions I made during that stage of my life. A ten-speed mountain bike, it was light years away from the old grids I'd used as a boy. In those days I'd thought three gears were pretty flash as I pedalled my paper round, throwing newspapers onto driveways or into doorways six days a week, wet or fine.

This new bike was a reason to get up in the morning, to get out on the country roads, biking through farmland, out to beaches before the heat of the day. Some days I'd ride up to eighty kilometres just for the sheer motion of pedalling to nowhere in particular. As well as exercise, it meant not having to face the sound of my solitary movements in the sparsely furnished flat. Every road in the district became familiar to me, as daily I explored in ever-widening circles.

In the end, however, it was necessary to face the silence of the empty flat. I visited the doctor, recognising I could not do this on my own. Something had turned the tap on and I didn't know how to turn it off. Shirley, the Buddhist counsellor, invited me to phone her every day, because I couldn't afford formal sessions at the clinic.

'Pat,' she told me, 'if you are going to cry, let yourself get on with it. You won't start to laugh until you've finished crying.' I phoned her almost daily for a month, and she was more help than I'd ever imagined I could need. All through that time I spent struggling to find reasons to live through another day, Shirley generously spent time talking with me on the phone. When it came time to end the call, she always used the same question.

'What are you going to do now?'

And I would tell her. 'Oh, I'll go for a bike ride,' or maybe,

'I'll go and buy some meat for dinner,' or 'I'm visiting Max and Marg.'

'Okay, phone if you need to talk tomorrow.' Only then would she hang up. And the phone would click. I'd go and do whatever it was I'd said I'd do.

Weeks passed. I wrote to my parents saying, 'If you don't hear from me everything is fine, I just need some time to myself.' After writing every week or second week for my entire adult life, I never wrote a letter to my mother again. Birthday and Christmas cards I did send, but that was it.

Throughout eight months in the flat, I woke in the morning to look toward the light coming through the bedroom window, checking the weather. The only object to be seen through the glass was a derelict tree stump. It had been brutally pruned some time before I rented the flat, and appeared dead. Through the winter months the stump remained unchanged. The calendar showed September and still no sign of life. Then one morning a slight movement of the wind caused a flicker of green to draw my attention to the window for a second look. A couple of brand new leaves were growing high up, against the grey bark of the naked stump. Over the next few days another leaf, then another, appeared. The stump was alive. I would wake and lie looking at the shine of light on leaves. Sometimes it still felt strange to wake alone, but the tree continued to sprout foliage, and I drew strength from its will to seek light. One old deciduous stump became my unlikely talisman, a living thing to seek out each day as I awoke. Now I can't even remember what species of tree it was.

Like the tree I was going to be okay. Month followed month, a time arrived to make new plans. There were options I needed to consider. Friends, some of whom had been helpful and generous, may have wondered what was going on. Ultimately, what others thought had little to do with work I had to get on with. I had to be strong enough to change habits that were self-destructive, and learn to live positively. Should I stay in Northland and buy a section where I could rough it until things improved? Should I leave town and start out somewhere else? What was it that would be most positive? Would I be able to get a job?

I'd spent years becoming skilled in avoiding what my own mind was telling me. Even before I left school I was doing some dumb things to please others—applying for a job at Seaview Mental Hospital for instance. I didn't take the job that was offered, but it was a close-run thing. I can't imagine what made me consider psychiatric nursing as a possible career. Mental illness was something to fear, that and the possibility of being locked away. Mum nurse-aided at Sunnyside Mental Asylum before marrying Dad in 1933. Sometimes she talked about patients she had nursed. There was one who really stuck in my mind.

'She was a poor thing,' said Mum. 'She'd take all her clothes off, and go out to the high barbed wire fence and hang herself on it like a crucifix.'

How young was I when first I heard that story? And what was I doing applying to work in a place with associations like that? So what if psychiatric treatment had changed? I was probably afraid of going off my head, more ready to believe the plot of *One Flew Over the Cuckoo's Nest* than to contemplate help for myself, or helping others. Even Mum could have done with some sort of treatment during her early valium years. But with her memories of Sunnyside intact, she was not going anywhere near treatment for what went on inside her head. That was successfully communicated to all of us kids. It certainly made an impression on me. Eventually, years later, I learned the hard way to leave others to play their manipulative games without me for company, to put the oxygen mask on myself first, before helping others. Without realising it, I'd spent the years before my fortieth birthday gasping for breath as my own resources dwindled.

The next time I saw my mother was three years after I'd fallen apart at the seams. By then I had shifted to Christchurch, and had driven up with Chris, and my sons, Andrew and Gareth. We caught the overnight ferry, arriving in Stratford on what was the evening in which she would die. Walking down the hospital corridor I passed her open door without recognising her and had to be called back to the room by the others. The emphysema had ravaged her body until very little of what we'd known of her was left. My brother Chris, my sons and I sat with her for a while, as she struggled for breath inside an oxygen mask. Her feverish eyes gazed across the blankets at Chris, thrilled to see him off the booze and looking well. Only later did I realise that really the boys and I didn't have to be there. Chris was the person she needed to see at that time. Somehow I'd spent my life trying so hard to please, it had escaped my notice that actually Chris was special to Mum in a way that I could never be.

Later that night after we were woken to be told Mum died at two a.m., and after we'd been down to see her in the hospital ward, I stood outside on the veranda of my parents' home. My farewells to my mother had taken place, and the rest of the family would be able to look after our father. It seemed at the time there was no reason to stay for the funeral. In the morning we set off home, back to Christchurch. My brothers and sisters might say we were all special in some way or another, each of us having a role to play in the family. That episode left me feeling entirely superfluous once I'd driven the car through the night to get my brother to his mother's bedside. Les Murray, the Australian poet, wrote 'the one in the family who is going to be a writer is always an only child', and there were times it could feel that way—the only child from somewhere else, an outsider. It was time to start making friends with the night sky, darkness, and the sound of my own laughter once more.

I read somewhere that working-class homes are more out in the open when family things go wrong, whereas middle-class people tend to be more hushed up, more aware of public appearances. My parents weren't particularly middle-class to my way of thinking, but they sure didn't appreciate their home life being public. In fact, my mother was not so much private as secretive in many ways. Many New Zealanders, of all classes, have grown up in families where violence is accepted as a matter of course, almost a sign that parents care enough to punish. There is more than physicality to violence. The effects of mental and emotional power struggles are much less talked about, and more difficult to see, but that does not mean they are less potent.

Excessive violence is too often excused. We fudge the truth. We hide behind facile statements, and say every situation is different, or that some things are better just left alone. Experience tells me that while some things are better just left to gather dust, it is also true that some events should be picked up, polished and given a bit of light. Gaps in our understanding of the past generate longings—whirlpools, or black holes in the kaleidoscope of events we place ourselves among as we grow and mature in search of an identity. Enough gaps and black holes among the galaxies of our dreams, and all we know is unrequited longing, and something I for one could not face.

Instead of going to Mum's funeral, I went home, to my house. This was where I learned, out of necessity, to live alone, finding a way to live that was mine. There were days when I'd have settled for a friendly smile, a breakfast with someone I felt comfortable with, or a few things waiting to be sown in the garden and maybe some eggs to gather from the chook house—or just sitting on the deck watching the birds fly past. Being alone was terrifying. There was no one to help, no one to do things for. After a while, having time on my hands gave me time to try some things out—Maori language classes, cooking new recipes, playing cricket again after years of no sport. And, as I had in Hokitika over ten years earlier, reading books that challenged my view of the world. It was in Christchurch that I read *The Aquarian Conspiracy,* and *The Unknown Craftsman* by Söetsu Yanagi. These books were positive without being prescriptive. I discovered Carl Jung and poets such as Gary Snyder and Seamus Heaney. Slowly I gained new perspectives, less desolate ways of looking at the world.

Yet when Loren Eiseley, an American philosopher, palae-ontologist and famous essayist says:

In a universe whose size is beyond human imagining, where our world floats like a dust mote in the void of night, men have grown inconceivably lonely. We scan the time scale and mechanisms of life itself for signs and portents of the invisible. As the only thinking mammals on the planet— perhaps the only thinking animals in the entire sidereal universe—the burden of consciousness has grown heavy on us. We watch the stars but the signs are uncertain—

97

I can see what he's getting at. My more positive approach to life had to be a cognitive practice, as the dark side was never far from bubbling through the surface.

If we dare to take ownership of our longings, what then? Is it just as simple as being alive? During my teenage years my mother used to remind me, 'Don't think I'm going to run after you. If you do, you've got another think coming, m'boy.'

'I'm not asking—'

'You've got to earn love from me. Now get out of my way, can't you see I'm busy.'

And we like to say 'names will never hurt you' as if language has no power. I've grown to believe words are everything when used toward children.

'If it wasn't for you bloody kids I'd be out of here,' my mother used to declare. It meant that I was to blame for her unhappiness. What else could it mean?

She would wait while we told her about an event we'd been to, or a film we'd seen. 'I would've liked to go to that,' she'd say eventually, without looking up from the embroidery she was working on. Once again, of course, it was my fault I didn't ask her.

When, during a fight with her while I was a teenager, she backed me up against the door, telling me 'none of the others have beaten me, so don't think for a minute you're going to', the choices were limited. As she looked up at me snarling, 'If you think so, you've got another think coming, my boy!', I looked down at her and capitulated. What a hollow victory. I'd never be 'her boy' but I backed off anyway. I had no intention of thumping her one, and nothing else would have stopped her desire for control.

My loving parents—they did the very best they could at the time. It would be unkind and self-indulgent to begrudge them that recognition. Another time, even a different place in the line-up of the seven children in the family, and my experience would have been very different. The older of my brothers and sisters can remember picnics and going to the river for a swim when Mum and Dad were younger. I don't. My younger brothers often went to the movies with Mum and Dad—after I left home. Each of my brothers and sisters would be able to assemble their own story of how things were for them, using examples to show both good and bad. That doesn't mean any of them had a better time of it, just different. My parents gifted me with a love of books, music and growing things—but, perhaps foolishly, the child in me wanted things they couldn't give.

At one point I belted Andrew and Gareth for something when they were eight and five or maybe a little younger, when the conflict—if there was one—was really between their mother and me. Realising that frightened me sufficiently to make me stop smacking. What it didn't do was give me another way of dealing with conflict, a substitute for the one I'd inherited. To be a person worthwhile in my own right there were things I had to change, and that had nothing to do with my parents. It took time for that message to sink in—another decade almost.

There is a saying that appears from time to time as one of those catch-all phrases the weekly magazines offer. You can blame your parents for a lot, but once you are fifty (or variously, forty or sixty) it is time to take responsibility for the person you are. When I moved to Christchurch from Northland in my fortieth year, it was time for me to stop the blaming, to accept the imperfections and longings in myself as well as in my parents—and then there was the task of getting on with the rest of my life.

In a journal kept in Northland well before my shaky world imploded, I'd taken note of a recurring dream. In the dream I lived in a cottage by myself. The cottage had a bay window and a garden. Things were in their right place. A pathway wound through the garden and led up to the cottage. There was light in the dream, and a lightness of being. At the time I'd laugh about what such a dream could mean as I recorded it, the same each time. Nothing could have been further from the way I lived, and nothing like it existed in the solutions I was fighting for to solve problems from day to day. When my wife said our life together was over, I felt she was being cruel. It was her rejecting me. Yet, here I was less than a year later, living alone in a real cottage, literally living the dream. The bay window looked out on a garden, from which I collected salad greens for my meals. A pathway lay beside the garden. Sure, this house had a demolition order on it, before I bought it, first reroofing, and then restoring it to a habitable level inside using recycled cupboards and kitchen fittings. The armchair in the tiny living room had plates of plywood beneath it to stop the legs going through the floor. Afternoon sunlight flooded the kitchen while I cooked. Shelves held my books and records, my spinning wheel sat ready to use at any time. The cottage of my dreams was a dump to look at, but it was mine.

To make a major life change is difficult, involving the adoption of different habits and, ultimately, thought patterns. In my case, I had to begin by learning to be less sarcastic, to remove the throwaway line of cynicism designed to get a laugh. 'What else can you expect from a loser,' when suggesting I could have done better, or, 'Of course you'd do it right,' when fielding criticism. A series of put-downs and evasions, touched with self-deprecating laughter, was no way to open myself to change. Once attention was drawn to my speech, I seemed to enter a bottomless pit. I've learned that ultimately we become the words we use, and the battle with sarcasm, half-truths, cynicism and prevarications took on huge importance as I tried to remake my world. Habits got picked apart at the seams as I realised that slinging off to gain laughs at someone else's expense, gossip, derogatory off-the-cuff comments, all cost the person that indulges them. Ah, words and the mystery of language, both our biggest asset and greatest liability when we deal with each other in any way beyond the superficial.

'It's not fair,' we'd complain to Dad.

'No,' he'd reply. 'It's dark.'

It was a revelation to realise that the way I spoke contributed to the way I felt, and to how my world turned out. We can literally talk ourselves into and out of being a particular person. We become what we speak.

I also had to find out who I wanted to be, without reflecting the desires of others. It meant learning to accept times of intense loneliness, days of solitude with my own critical self. Especially during the cottage years, a healing of sorts did take place, starting so deep inside me that I wasn't even sure it was there on a bad day. Yet inevitably, it seems now, there came a time to leave Christchurch, to strike out with something new. 'The Sully', as my cottage was christened, had done her job and the holes in the floor were becoming an urgent and expensive task to be attended to by someone with more money than I had. Besides, I had new adventures in mind, new energy and skills to draw on, and to try out.

Over twenty years since leaving Christchurch, life has changed shape. What is old has been given different meaning, what is new arrives with recognition of longing as a call for transformation, or at least a need to act.

'Hope is a moral responsibility,' Michael Cathcart says on the radio this morning.

'He's right,' I hear Catherine saying. From where we sit, looking out to the mountains, with trees sprouting new growth and clouds due to dump more spring rain, I have to agree.

'Yes, hope is what gets us out of bed in the morning.' Later, in my study, I return to what I'd written earlier. It's still true enough. My study is lined with book shelves, and the spinning wheel is in the living room where I can use it any evening. Outside, a drive winds through trees, a path leads out to the garden and chook house.

Winter closes down our paddocks, turning grass brown with frost burn, soil soggy and cold with rain. Dark shadows from the low-angled sun lie along the fencelines, if the sun should choose to shine at all. The hare will still run, as if there are no seasons. He can be seen from time to time, probably hungry and possibly cold, but from where I watch he is free to do what he does best—run. A hare runs in straight lines, chews back trees or branches of trees growing into his flight path. He prefers clear sight lines, and it is easy to identify his work as I look at the neat forty-five degree angle of the cut branch—new growth lying on the ground where the hare let it drop to rot. If some disturbance raises a hare, he will run, before returning to his set by way of a wide circular route. Our fences mean nothing to him—he lives by slipping through fences, loping over roads, and criss-crossing farm tracks to be again where he was yesterday. Our human mind can be as predictable as the hare's pathways, revisiting the past, to which we return time and time again, to scratch at the same places. On another afternoon he will not be running, but might rest out of the wind, snug against a random clump of cocksfoot, facing the sun and watching for sign or listening for sound that may let him know he's safe a little longer.

But the hare is just being himself. As far as we can tell, he knows no other way. There he lies this afternoon, out on the slope, oblivious to the fact that I am watching him, or maybe tucked inside the hare-zen of feeling safe because I've watched him this way for days and no harm has come down the path with my presence. There are things that I used to claim would prevent me from living in the moment—this moment when the hare rises, to browse a little in the last weak rays of sunlight, nibbling at vegetation the same russet colour as his own fur. I can no longer project blame for my state of mind on what others do or think. Like the running hare, I can choose to flee, or lie hoping my camouflage is up to the task of protection, but the choice, when it arises, is mine. There are days when it is possible to feel I am as close to this buck-toothed running machine, the subject of my admiration despite his wide eyes and big ears, as I ever was to those intimate strangers, my parents. On other days I flounder about, intent on vague longings for what might have been. Yet I know when I am in one of those indulgent self-pitying moments, that I am on tracks where the scent has grown cold. That time to change the past is in the past. Where grass once bent with prints of someone making their tentative way along an ancient trail, there are now only stories to be told—hopefully with compassion and a desire for understanding. My business is to do what the day provides, just like the hare, as his teeth cut back another branch out there among the olives we planted.

A bookish thing

In my mind there is no time when I was unable to read. Books have always been there. Yet I have no memory of being read to. Instead there was nothing, then there were nightmares caused by chance reading of anything I could get my hands on.

The book to give me my first memory of bad dreams is also the first book I remember reading. *Spear and Stockwhip*, written by Australian author R.H. Graves, uses cattle droving as the setting for a boy's adventure yarn and deals in stereotypes, a book without great distinction. For over fifty years I remembered it, because a teenage boy gets speared by aborigines to die a lingering death in the great Australian outback. *Spear and Stockwhip* was my brother's book, and John was not only four years older than me but also much more capable of not caring about a bit of blood and guts. A couple of years ago my brother Keith who lives in Melbourne picked up a second-hand copy of the book and sent it to me, after we'd been talking casually about early memories. It turns out that none of the five teenagers who feature in the adventure actually died, and that the adult character who was speared in the story died straight off. And, more to the point, why was the book so important in the first place?

Most people seem to have a particular picture book as an

earliest reading memory. Catherine, for instance, remembers *Babar the Elephant*, created by Jean de Brunhoff. My son Andrew lists a number of picture books, including one or two written by Dr Seuss, or *Tintin* by Hergé. Someone else has *Where the Wild Things Are* in mind, remembering the fabulously scary pictures of Maurice Sendak. On my own shelves is a very dilapidated copy of *Milly Molly Mandy*. Paul Gallico's *The Snow Goose* is there, having been rescued from the ravages of childhood handling. The copy of *The Ugly Duckling*, featuring wonderful illustrations by Will Nickless, I keep, in spite of missing pages and a cover that barely holds on down the spine.

How many times did I take that Hans Christian Andersen classic from the shelves to read to Andrew and Gareth when they were small? Even then, it was very much the worse for wear. While these books have obviously been handled countless times, I have no memory of them from my own childhood, despite childish writing claiming them as mine inside the front cover. Nor do I remember being read to each evening at bedtime, the way I did to Andrew and Gareth almost every night of their childhood. That is, until their mother and I separated, when Andrew was eight years old and Gareth younger still. Is it bitter or sweet to recall reading to my little boys once they were tucked into bed? One would lie with a cuddly, the other thumb sucking—the sucking would grow gentle as the story progressed. Finally the thumb and lips parted just a tiny bit, as Gareth first, and then eventually Andrew, would fall asleep. The cuddly would have dropped onto the pillow, and I would be sitting reading to myself about a wicked wolf, a friendly ghost, or some other make-believe world where they would always end up safe anyway.

Instead of calm bedtimes in the bunks, I remember other things. Lantern light through a half-shut door at Inangahua, and a whole lot of us in a double bed together, while in

105

the next room a party and singing were taking place. Very occasionally Dad was there, taking his false teeth out to make funny faces while telling us stories he messed with— *Little Hood Redding Ride*, or *Poor Little Willy T'Hell*. He would have us giggling and begging for more. And then Mum's urgent voice from the sitting room—'Don't you go getting those kids all stirred up, Jack!'—while we were wild with laughter and eager for more, bouncing round with sleep the last thing on our minds.

We did read in bed, stories of struggle and heroism, books taken out of school libraries about wagon trains and sailing ships, or trappers in Canada. Schoolboy stories of winning the cricket game for the first eleven, after a season of disgrace and loss. Sometimes the film version mixes with the book. Smoke and flames and terrified neighing of horses in a stable fire do not belong to the printed version of *Black Beauty* which was a Christmas present from my oldest sister Lesley in 1953, but to the film we saw at Inangahua Junction earlier, back in 1949. Flames and films affected me strongly as a child. My second sister, Elena, tells the story of going to *Bambi* in Gore, the first film I ever went to. When the forest fire started and the animals were all running to escape, apparently I got so distraught I had to be taken home. Mum used to tell a story from her childhood about a fire and the memory of her father cutting the wall out with an axe to get it under control.

Other stories we listened to on the radio, especially during children's request sessions, which added music or particular voices to the printed word. Bing Crosby's voice is firmly imprinted with the story of *The Littlest Donkey*, while I have no memory of who read *The Happy Prince*, or *Flick the Little Fire Engine*. *The Ugly Duckling* story is linked to the voice of comedian Danny Kaye who acted the part of Hans Christian Andersen, and sang a song version of the 'ugly duckling'. Dramatic music and the sound of planes and guns featured in *The Snow Goose* as it played on request sessions many times during my childhood. That story is a mix of nature fable, love story and homage to Dunkirk, site of the Allies' retreat from France in 1940. The fact that the book was published in 1940 and we listened to the recorded version soon after the end of the Second World War doubtless added poignancy to its reception in many homes.

Books were a place in which I could imagine myself to be the hero, involved at the centre of every excitement, or any dangerous escapade. Of course, just as we all played cards or did jigsaws, so books were read by everyone in the family. They still are, as far as I know, with books of interest being a comfortable topic of conversation during infrequent phone calls. These days, however, my brothers and sisters are spread out round New Zealand and Australia, and there is none of the round-robin swapping of books that used to take place when we were kids at Ross, which is where I first remember reading. Our shift to New Plymouth led to the discovery of public libraries, and use of them has continued to this day.

I have a suspicion Dad read more as a young man than he did after he married, or maybe after there were so many kids around. Certainly the books he talked about when I was a teenager were ones he read many years earlier. Upton Sinclair's *The Jungle*, *And Quiet Flows the Don* by the Russian author Mikhail Sholokhov—they were both reflections of his desire for social justice. I can still hear the echo of his voice.

'They talk about justice,' his tone scathing. 'Those bastards. They deal in usury. And who pays in the end?' The question, and the pause, would be rhetorical. 'Wage earners, that's who pays.' So often his sense of social concern was directed at 'them', the generic face of what was wrong but too big to put right. The Social Credit Party got his vote for years because of his disgust with capitalism. While I would listen to what he said, it was best not to try to actually discuss politics with him. Due to his volatile readiness to take offence over

107

a differing opinion, what I thought was better kept under wraps. Not that I disagreed with him about interest, lending and the issue of usury. Back then I was every inch an idealist, but lacked his anger, the cause of which I remain ignorant. Growing up in what must have been some poverty after his father died, and his experience of the Great Depression, may certainly have aroused his interest in socialism and there are certainly hints of socialist leanings in the way he talked.

I have not read Upton Sinclair, and only Sholokhov short stories. My interests have not always coincided with those of my father. I don't know if he ever read it, but there is another book on my shelves that does remind me of Dad. *Dear Fatherland, Rest Quietly* is by the photographer Margaret Bourke-White, who was among the earliest press corps personnel to see, in 1945, what war had brought to Germany, as the Allies pushed forward in the final weeks before achieving victory in Europe. While her graphic black and white illustrations, of destroyed German cities and the results of concentration camps such as Buchenwald, may have lost some impact through familiarity, it is not difficult to imagine what effect they would have had, first in *Life* magazine during 1945, then with the book's publication in 1946.

Dad was aware of the destruction of Dresden, and the carpet bombing campaigns of the Allies against Germany. He was just as quick to condemn the inhumanity of that activity as he was the Holocaust.

'What justification,' he would say, 'is there in flattening a city? That fire bomb in Dresden, killing the women and children—what had they done?' And always the questions to which there were no answers. He was right, but what could his kids do about it in the 1960s?

'Why would they do that?' he would ask. And of course, we did not know. For us the bombing of Dresden was less of a threat than the atomic bombs being exploded on Mururoa.

The sunsets after an atmospheric test or even during Australian bushfires were phenomenal, climbing vividly on dust clouds high into the atmosphere, turning skies west of Greymouth into other-worldly colour charts as dusk brought the sun down over the sea. Dad was prepared to condemn atomic bombs as well, but for him, they did not have the vivid intensity of the recalled horror of the blanket bombing of European cities.

By the time I was aware of what Dad might be reading, he was more likely to be checking out a magazine such as *NZ Gardener*, *Field & Stream*, or *Outdoors*. His willingness to read about the world narrowed, and his focus turned towards shooting and fishing magazines. His was becoming more insular, until even the *National Geographic* subscription was allowed to lapse. Books were still easy gifts for his birthday or Christmas, however, and Mum used to buy him a topical selection that catered for his interests. In 1956, it was *Fly Fishing in New Zealand* by George Ferris, then in 1961, Peter Scott's autobiographical *Eye of the Wind*.

Unlike Dad, as we grew older, Mum read more. Her workload diminished each time another child left home, so that by the time we lived in Greymouth and we three younger boys entered our teens, she spent hours every day reading. Not that she stopped doing other things. Oh no! Mum would sit smoking a cigarette she had rolled herself, reading a novel and knitting a jersey for one of us, or perhaps a pair of booties for a grandchild. No trouble at all. Or she would be crocheting a doily or tea cosy as a present. She always seemed to have several things on the go—a book for the kitchen and one by her bed, crochet and knitting, or embroidery of one sort or another lined up beside the sofa in the kitchen, and more in the sunny spare room where she could sit if we were all out of the house at work or school. Her book collection consisted of Georgette Heyer, Victoria Holt and other light historical romances, Denis Wheatley and his soft-option occult witchcraft brew, endless detective yarns by the likes of John Creasey, and the 'Bony' series of Arthur Upfield set in the Australian outback. E.V. Timms and Laurens Van Der Post were also on the shelves. She developed a taste for travel books, and read about the pyramids of Egypt, and South America. Books were bought, borrowed, swapped and accumulated to gather dust anywhere there was a shelf to put them.

She would talk to John about his thrillers, or cheap American detective novels. He loved trash such as Carter Brown's pulp fiction. She was happy to pass on what she read as well, or to spend time with him, until he met the love of his life and there was a fundamental parting of the ways. No girl was ever going to be quite good enough for any of Mum's boys.

John and books were a different story for Dad though. He had no idea how John could read a book in a couple of hours. That problem escalated to the point where John would be quizzed.

'You can't read that fast,' Dad would say, ready for a scrap. He picked up *Riders of the Purple Sage* from where John had tossed it to one side. Dad had read Zane Grey westerns as a youngster, so he had some knowledge of the plots in most of the them. He'd flick through the book until he hit on a familiar scene. 'What happens . . .', and he'd ask some ridiculous questions of detail. John would, of course, answer them correctly. Dad would probe for any flaws in recall of plot or characterisation, and end up frustrated and looking foolish. John read with a photographic memory and so fast there was never enough print round the house to hold off his tendency toward boredom. Elena and Chris also had photographic recall of anything they read. Their idea of studying for exams was to skim through a book or two the night before, and still score good marks. Yet they all loved books and the act of reading. Later on Chris would also spend hours talking with Mum about books they had both read. That was something I never did. I have no idea whether Keith did much chatting with her or not, but he was different anyway. Although he read Gerald Durrell's wonderfully playful wildlife stories, and still does, I don't remember him reading very much, especially once he got into music.

We were given guitars when he was ten and I was fourteen. He took his off somewhere while I mucked around with this thing in my hands. Half an hour later he was back.

'Listen to this,' he suggested, bending over the instrument. The bass notes of 'Ghost Riders in the Sky' twanged across the veranda. Without waiting to receive applause, he said, 'And this is how you tune it,' all excited. I was never once able to tune that instrument, and in the end gave it away, without ever understanding why I was quite so hopeless at it. Before Keith turned fifteen he was playing in bands at dances, before he was eighteen he was gigging in pubs up and down the West Coast. The answer in my case was simple really. I had poor hearing from a young age, but adapted well enough for the lack not to be picked up. To other people if I got the wrong end of the stick I was just a lazy listener, and with the guitar they thought I couldn't be bothered.

Keith just loved that guitar. While I found it was very easy to disappear into books, Keith didn't have time. He'd walk in from school, dump his bag in his room and pick up his guitar.

'Hey Keith,' I'd say, tossing a cricket ball in the air at the weekend, 'do you want to have a few catches?' Nothing doing.

'Keith!' He'd look up from his playing. Before I'd get the question out for the second time, he'd be strumming, or picking a tune. He'd have a song in his head and barely register my existence. Up until I left home, he was to all intents and purposes absent—sitting in the room all right, but never there. He was more likely to know The Hollies' latest hit song than what he'd had for dinner that night. The guitar became part of his physical being.

Quite early on, I went off on different tangents, reading stuff that didn't interest anyone else round the house. When I started reading books about biblical matters, and the efficacy of prayer, for instance, as a sixteen-year-old, I was on my own. While I'm not sure anybody really cared what I thought in one sense, there was a party line to adhere to, and independence of opinion or thought were not welcome in the kitchen. It was fine to read for facts and stories, but ideas were a different matter altogether.

Mum used the same stock phrases that seem to have been shared with many other mothers of that postwar generation. Boys had to be kept in line, and she was just the person for the job.

'Stop moaning or I'll give you something to moan about,' she'd say. 'Blessed is he that expecteth nothing.' Or, 'Don't you go getting ideas above your station.' As if I could, when I was prepared to put a book on lay-by and pay it off at sixpence a week, because I surely wouldn't be getting it otherwise. As a young person I did not have the mind to reason things out: instead, I just knew what I wanted to do next.

At Greymouth Library I raided the shelves at random, often bringing home books that set me off on thoughts about what I could do or be. Reading Pierre La Mure's novels *Moulin Rouge* and *Clair de Lune,* about Henri de Toulouse-Lautrec and Claude Debussy respectively, it immediately became important to go to university and study art after I left school. Now I see that ambition resulted from seeds fertilised years earlier and directly involved a love of art. *Moulin Rouge* and the picture of artistic Parisian life only reignited an idea I had buried. My school projects over the years had amply demonstrated the fact that I had always liked drawing, copying or painting as well as books containing illustrations. Art was little more than kindling waiting for a catalyst to set it alight. My response to books and the ideas in them led to the biggest falling out I had with Mum.

In Rotorua, as a twelve- or thirteen-year-old, one afternoon I went to a friend's home. His mother was a painter, and for a couple of hours she let us use her water colours, splashing paint around under her guidance on the best paper I'd ever had the chance to paint on. I had no idea, before that afternoon, of the way quality water colour paper could absorb colour without buckling and sucking the vibrant life out of the pigment. An hour or two with good paint and quality paper opened my mind to a different world. Of course I had to go home wildly enthusiastic about the paints and paper, and declaring I had to buy some. Probably I also let slip that we never had paints that good at home. Naturally enough, I was refused permission to go to that friend's house again.

'People like that have got more money than they know what to do with,' was my mother's final word. 'Them, and their two-car garage. You're not going back and that's that.'

I did buy some good water colours with my paper-run money. A couple of years later at school in Greymouth I even studied art for School Certificate by correspondence against the advice of my parents and form teacher. They felt art could not be seen as a career option. In sixth form when I could not take art, one of the teachers urged me to aim for university, to stay on into a fifth year sitting bursary exams to try and get a studentship. At university I would be in a position to study history, English or art. To suggest that my mother was opposed to the idea drastically understates the case. She visited the school, bailed up the principal and let him know in no uncertain terms how things stood, telling him that teacher was to stop causing upset and disruption in our household.

There was to be no art school or university for me if my

113

mother had her way. The previous year I had painted a big water colour for my School Certificate course—a man on his knees in a dinghy with a huge wave bearing down on him. In memory that image is still powerful. Maybe because of that my mother had asked her Rawleigh's man, Toss Woollaston, if I should go to university and study art. He had already written about his scorn for Ilam Art School, but was probably the only artist Mum knew.

'It's a waste of time to go anywhere near the place,' was his reply.

I'd like to say I didn't give up without a fight. Even if it meant getting tossed out like John did, when he decided he was marrying a Catholic girl. But I was not John. I did go to university to study art, but it was not in defiance of my mother. With Catherine's encouragement I finally studied at the Massey University School of Fine Arts when I was over sixty years of age. By then Mum was long gone, Toss Woollaston knighted and famous for his landscape painting, and Denise, the love of John's life, was a widow. John died unexpectedly of a heart attack when he was only fifty-four.

The morning after John's funeral, Keith talked to me about the Greymouth years. We sat on beer crates, in the early sun of a Wairarapa day, a bit like strangers who have heard a lot about each other. He had no real memories of what it had been like at all, as if he'd disappeared inside the lyrics of one of his songs. My own image of that time had narrowed to a scene enacted night after night in the years before I left home.

I'd walk into the house at 10 Smith Street in Greymouth after school. She'd be sitting in the kitchen, on a sofa back against the wall not far from the coal range, peeling potatoes or otherwise preparing vegetables for that night's meal. There was a roll-your-own cigarette threading a veil of smoke across her features on its way toward the ceiling, her lank dark hair, clipped back from her forehead, and inevitably there was an apron—or 'pinny' as she called it—tied round her waist. Most often her greeting would be subdued, and I'd ask what she wanted done. Firewood, the coal scuttle, shopping, there always seems to have been something that needed doing before the evening meal, served when Dad got home from work some time after five.

Each week there was shopping for groceries. Once I put the shopping baskets on the scales down at the railway station, and found I was carrying home nearly thirty pounds of groceries. Mum would write a shopping list and have it waiting when I walked in after school. With four teenage boys in the house, keeping food in front of us was a major task. Even for the simplest of items I'd need a list. My memory could not handle the least of requirements, so messages were always a little fraught. In a house where people routinely read *Wisden's Cricket Almanac* and memorised scores or all manner of statistics, or where any phone numbers were carried in people's heads, I was subject to derision. Dad was still memorising new Masonic ritual in his eighties, and knew poems from school days. While he could lie in the bath letting it get cold while rehearsing lines most men read from the text rather than recited from memory, I was unable to rote-learn ten lines of Shakespeare for School Certificate, even after trying for three months. So lists were the thing, lists and 'Shank's pony'.

Without a car, we walked or biked everywhere, and that meant carrying things like shopping bags home each week. For a time, with Mum crook, Dad and John working, Chris liable to throw a tantrum if he was asked to take a single book back to the library, and Keith still a bit young, I was it. If someone was needed to go down town or to do whatever needed doing, I'd have to get home from school to do the job concerned. So after practice for cricket or hockey, it was home to chores, then homework. I was never secure enough in my school work to muck around. It all sounds a rather drab existence. I'm sure there were times of foolishness or play, but my memories are, for whatever reason, tinged with the drudgery of grinding on to get through school, helping at home—and trying to cope with suppressed hormones that would dearly love to have expressed themselves.

Mum set up camp in the kitchen. It was there she had her long talks with my brothers John and Chris about the woes of the world, and the Denis Wheatley novels they all read, or travel books, or the mock-Tibetan stories of Lobsang Rampa. By the time late afternoon came round, the sun had left the kitchen, it was dark, but warmed by the stove. Home from school, we entered it through a room where dishes were washed and food was stored, plus what always seemed to be lots of other stuff. To go further into the house we went through the dining room, which was used only if we were all eating together, otherwise we ate at the kitchen table that was covered with a plastic tablecloth. Those were also years when Mum had real health problems a lot of the time. She and Dad were not getting on so well. If I heard it once I heard it a dozen times, Mum storming from the kitchen seething with frustration about something I was too young to understand. Slam!

'Get on with your homework!'—a parting shot from the other side of the door

Half an hour later a placatory cup of tea could be taken to where she skulked in bed. Often enough she'd be there sucking away on a square of chocolate from the blocks she secreted in her bedside drawer, while reading some escapist novel from the library. Then Dad would arrive home from the pub wanting to talk.

By the time I was twelve, it was part of my life to buy books on lay-by. With my sixpences and shillings, I would get a volume put aside and return week after week until it was paid for and mine to own. I still have my *Commonwealth and Empire Annual* from 1957, with its black and white photographs and articles covering just about everything to do with the monarchy and the loyal colonies. By then I knew that books held a key to something for me. I just didn't know what it was.

In 1963 I left home for Teachers' College in Christchurch. There were textbooks, and novels to read by Steinbeck, Hemingway, John Wain or Lynne Reid Banks—but not for long. Within four years I was farming, and scavenging any reading matter I could, while studying farming by correspondence to make up for my lack of practical experience. A couple of years later I was the librarian at Hokitika.

The farming life ended rather suddenly, and getting work in Hokitika was a fluke. After ending up in hospital for a fortnight with viral meningitis, I needed time for recuperation. First there was a stay with friends for a short time, then a visit to look after my father-in-law who was ill. At one point in my stay he had his first fall. I rushed to where he lay collapsed on the floor of the bathroom. As I went to pick him up his eyes caught mine.

'I'm buggered aren't I?' he said. 'I'm buggered.'

By the time I went back home shortly after, he was in need of nursing care for his illness which was destined not to last much longer. I went back to Blackwater and the farm, and through winter tried to think about what I could do next. One wet day, just for something to do, I drove into Ikamatua and bought a newspaper. In the situations vacant the job at Hokitika was advertised. I applied, and went down for the interview soon after. I had to take Andrew with me for some reason, and he played round the office and under the desk while I was interviewed by a pipe-smoking town clerk, whose informality went with a sense of humour that was able to deal easily with a toddler getting into his bookshelves of legal tomes during a job interview. Before long we had moved to Hokitika and I started the job I was to grow into as if I was born for it. For the first time, books were to be more than pleasant recreation in the evening. I dealt with them all day long. Matching a borrower with what they may like reading, or find helpful, is a skill any small-town librarian needs and one I developed rapidly. There was a role for me among the shelves, and being a bookish boy would prove worthwhile after all. It was as if out of the illness and loss of the farm, something good happened, and I was once more on my way somewhere with hope.

In an itinerant working life, I've spent more time being a librarian than teacher or farmer. Yet I'd like to think all the possum shooting, truck driving, scallop sorting, firewood cutting, building and other bits and pieces, have helped me be a librarian more fit to deal with the public.

'You've got the common touch,' was how Mrs Chamberlain, who had herself been a volunteer librarian previously, put it in those early Hokitika days. As she realised the ambiguity of her statement, she blushed.

'I'll take that as a compliment,' I reassured her. 'See what y'think of this,' I suggested, giving her a brand new copy of Arthur Hailey's *Airport* to take home and read because I reckoned she'd enjoy it.

Essentially my arrival as Hokitika librarian stemmed from a moment in 1952 when my sister Lesley did something unexpected. She gave me a book. It was an extraordinary gift. A fragile green volume, taped together with faded elastoplasts, I still have it. My *Wild Life of the World* has several pages of index missing, but the text is intact, though tattered. It is inscribed 'to Pat with love from Les for your eighth birthday 22/8/52'. There are 382 pages of illustrated text, and for Lesley to buy the book in her first year of paid work must have been a considerable extravagance. Certainly the following year she was more restrained, buying me the copy of *Black Beauty* in a standard plain edition. Still, the effort had been made. The text must have been beyond my eight-year-old comprehension, but the photographs are still vivid nearly sixty years later, their black and white clarity intact. On every double-page spread there is at least one illustration, and often two, with many of them full page. Recently I was talking to my sister about her generosity, and she told me that our mother had been upset at the expense of the gesture. I can believe it.

Over fifty years later the mystery, in turning the next page to see what is there, persists. Second-hand bookshops draw me as if the only book I will ever need to buy is just through the door. For twenty years I have reviewed books for small town newspapers, and still enjoy the feel of crisp new pages. I am a bibliophile, with more desire for books than money to spend on them, or time to read them all.

And lurking in the background there has always been one book that seemed to come closer to my longings than any other. *The Old Man and the Boy,* written by Robert Ruark, a favourite book throughout my adult life, has been part of me so long I don't even remember when I first read it. Appearing in 1957, it was written when Ruark was at the height of his popularity and writing powers. Perhaps it was lying round the house after being given to my father as a present, or I got it out of the library. I have read it several times since.

In the book Ruark writes about growing up in rural North Carolina, and time spent with his grandfather. They hunt squirrels, deer, rabbits and all manner of bird life. Together they fish in the rivers and sea. Throughout the book, the 'Old Man' imparts wisdom, talking about everything from Shakespeare to training a 'coon' dog. In some ways the writing encapsulates the way of life I had a glimpse of as a small boy living at Ross in South Westland. Ruark captured the romance of boyhood lived outdoors and also captured my capacity to long for what I had never had.

Not long after we arrived in the Wairarapa I hunted out the second-hand bookshops. It was time I bought a copy of 'my' book. Asking around, nobody had a copy. What's more they'd never heard of Robert Ruark, let alone of *The Old Man and the Boy*. Then my luck changed: a second-hand shop in Upper Hutt was owned by a man who at least knew of the book I was talking about.

'Leave it with me,' he said. 'Give us your phone number. Every so often a book comes through that somebody wants particularly.'

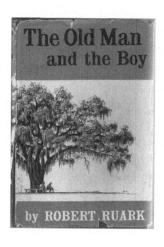

Somewhat sceptically I wrote down the details, and promptly forgot about it. Almost a year later I got a phone call. The book was waiting for me to pick up next time I passed through the Hutt. I paid the ten dollars and brought my prize home to read.

Robert Ruark, at the time of writing his most popular book, was seriously drinking himself to death, killing himself by the glassful. If his childhood was such a model of balance and self-development, he would have grown up more emotionally robust. I can see now that the book is an exercise in nostalgia, beautifully and powerfully written, but essentially an alcoholic's backward glance toward a golden time, or series of special memories. The book also expresses sadness, sorrow for what is lost, and a sensitive boy's longing to escape aspects of what a harsh life has since dealt out to him. By writing the 'everlasting summer' of his childhood, Ruark was able to escape the darkness of war, incomprehensible acts of violent men, and re-enter a rural existence that has since been swallowed by modernity and development. That 'promised land', where good guys prevail to be rewarded with a beautiful damsel, and where justice ensures pure thoughts, is an illusion, or at best a rosy-tinted nostalgia, in which it can be unhealthy to spend too much time. The book is full of conversations that are, by definition, a fictional recall of the past. It feels difficult to pass judgement in this way, almost as if I am betraying an article of faith.

What strikes me now is that the brilliant dialogue between man and boy, and the action on the river bank, or in the fields with the gundogs, were adhering to an American dream of living off the land with freedom to roam. The pivotal issue for the author is found in a single sentence—'I suppose everybody has one particular chunk of time he wishes he could get back and live all over again.' Those words encapsulate the reason *The Old Man and the Boy* was ever written.

I am more prepared to see flaws in the book than I once was, but it still owns a certain charm if one identifies with outdoor living, shooting and fishing, or even mucking around in the countryside. There is no harm in escapism when we understand that is what we are indulging in. Yet inside Ruark's idyllic prose web lies an unbearable sense of the loss of childhood innocence. I can see now that the reason the book got under my skin is because I also wanted an 'Old Man' in my life.

My father was just beginning to spend nights out with his father on the rabbit trapping lines, to go fishing and shooting with him, to live beside him—when the man killed himself.

Dad painted a picture of time shared doing arduous work—the setting of gin traps at the mouths of rabbit burrows, snares along fences using flexible wire to make the noose, getting a short sleep after the traps were set before going round them, then resetting the traps and bringing in the rabbits to skin before another sleep, then round the traps once more before dawn.

Obviously the occasions when he was able to go out with his father were precious to him. It was the sharing that shone through, a boy doing grown-up stuff with his father. I knew what it was to be with Dad when we went out fishing, and the once or twice we went shooting, so it was easy to comprehend what he missed—at one level. With our constant shifting from one place to another, I found Dad would change, depending on what opportunities the next place had to offer in the way of fishing or shooting. For different reasons I spent my childhood, after being at Ross, longing for Dad to be again what he had been there. We just never lived in another place where that was possible. What Ruark wrote about was also a world, shared with adults, that I only had hints of when I first read it. Apart from my father's one or two stories about his own father, or the rare visits of my other grandfather, a large part of my childhood story is imagined. I wanted more written on the pages of my daily existence, and went to imagined places to find it.

While Ruark wrote about his grandfather I think in some way I transformed that text into a story about my Dad's father, who was already dead. What the psychological technicalities are, I'm not so sure, but I somehow took ownership of Dad's sense of loss while still a child. When his father killed himself, Dad was ten years old, so for him that loss was tangible. When Ruark's book came into my hands, although I had yet to learn the facts about that longing of my father, I must have sensed something. Any suicide has elements of betrayal, guilt and blame mixed into the aftermath. Dad had all those feelings, I realise now, but they were never expressed in context. My loss was a phantom more than a reality—after all, I had my father alive, right beside me a lot of the time.

Perhaps back when I received that copy of *The Old Man and the Boy* from the Upper Hutt book shop might have been the right time to take it to Stratford and talk to Dad. I didn't do that, and he has died. As with any death in a family, things change afterwards. My older brother John had also died. All my uncles are gone as well. I have become 'the old man', the oldest surviving son in the extended family. With the passage of time, some things are held onto, some have to be let go.

Another book I have had on my shelves, only to give away two or three copies since it appeared in 1996, is *I Don't Want to Talk About It* by Terence Real. Each time I bought a copy, out the door it went. Put very briefly, the book tells the story of covert depression following trauma, showing how emotional states are passed from one generation of men to the next. I gave one copy to Gareth and his partner, but my son refuses to read it. Fathers are not supposed to tell their sons the stories of their fears and longings; they are just expected to slog on, to cope with life the best they can from day to day.

It is time to leave Robert Ruark and his grandfather. Now I am the grandfather, and there are children who may visit one day. I have books to read to them, and stories to tell. Perhaps just as importantly, I also have books to remind me that my past is just a story, one of many different versions of similar stories.

In *A Lie About My Father* author John Burnside tells how during the mid-1990s in Upper New York State he picked up a hitch-hiker, 'Mike', who asks about his father. 'He died,' is Burnside's reply. It is partly a lie, and Burnside uses the impulse given by that act of lying to write about his troubled and violent childhood and the compulsive lying of his father, who himself had had a violent and abandoned childhood. Books are a way of sharing information, sometimes inexact, and only with skilled word use, more than approximate—yet for all that, better than nothing. Words are thought to be precise in their meanings, but our stories sometimes use words as imprecise tools to reach out to readers. When Burnside writes about the time he realised he told a 'lie' rather than confront the story of his father, I can understand the feeling involved. The facts may well be adjusted to avoid getting at the truth within the story. But the story remains. Telling stories is often trying to make sense of something a little beyond our understanding, to the edge of our acceptance of ourselves. They may be reaching out to someone else, who may be our father, grandfather or grandson, and maybe a total stranger. I am glad Burnside wrote about his 'lie' and his father, because his experience has helped me think about mine—do I mean my lies, my father and his evasions, or my experience? If I follow Burnside, the book will be about truths, at times deeper truths, that lie beneath the stories.

The writer Peter Hooper once told me he had decided to read no more new books. At his age, he needed to deal with the fact that he should use any time he had left with only the best books he knew.

'There is so much wisdom already on my shelves,' he said. 'I think it is time to spend the remainder of my life trying to get more from what I know are great and wise books.'

'I don't think I've reached that stage,' I replied.

'You will,' he assured me.

But I have not done so yet, and I have no way of knowing how much time I have left. I will go on reading books, both old and new, making friends with some and discarding others. I'd like to think that the idea of turning the next page just for the hell of finding what might be there, perhaps the hope that it will change my life, might never leave me. It is a bookish thing.

Tararuas as Gallipoli: suite

Buy three sheets of pressed board, and cut them in half, so that each measures 1200 mm x 1200 mm. Paint the entire surface of each piece with white acrylic undercoat until a complete seal is achieved. Lastly, coat the surface to be used for the paintings with gesso. Allow the gesso to dry thoroughly and place the boards along the wall where you will be working.

Before I put aside my paint brushes, one last painting is to be finished. *Tararuas as Gallipoli* will consist of five of the 1200 mm x 2100 mm panels. Easily the largest work I've ever painted, this work will require over six metres of wall space to hang it. Life drawing is finished for this semester, the studio is vacant—though upstairs can be stifling and hot—and I should be able to work out of everyone's way. A row of student desks pushed against the wall should hold the board sections at the right height on which to paint. There is nothing stopping me . . .

It's late 2003, and I am well on the way with the Jack Dunn exhibition, having already finished after a false start, landscapes now discarded. The abstract works of the *Gallipoli Suite* which everyone likes to say are influenced by Hotere or McCahon, the *Offshore*, and *Night Sky over Gallipoli* paintings, are all stored away, drying. A collection of fourteen poems I've written complementing the *Gallipoli Suite* is waiting for inclusion in the catalogue.

Painting Gallipoli started at a poetry reading in Masterton within sight of the peaks I was now painting. My friend Michael Harlow was passing through town with a 'Words on Wheels' tour, so I went in to hear him and the other travelling wordsmiths read at the library. The event passed on to the inevitable cup of tea and mingling. At one point Michael introduced me to Chris Pugsley, author of *Gallipoli: The New Zealand Story.*

'Are you related to Jack White from Stratford?' Chris asked after a few minutes.

'He's my father. Why?'

'I recorded him a couple of weeks ago. He said he had a son down this way and you look a bit like him.'

'Recorded him?'

'I wanted to talk to him about Jack Dunn.'

'Who is Jack Dunn?'

And so I first heard of Private John Robert Dunn, who died fighting at Gallipoli in 1915. He was one of the Anzacs.

That meeting with Chris took place on 16 November 1993. On 25 April 2005, my exhibition *Gallipoli: In Search of a Family Story* opened, featuring a decade of research into the story of Jack Dunn. It was a decade of learning of many other things about my family's past as well.

In late 2003, I had no idea *Each field its own story* was still to be painted. The thought would have terrified me. Sometimes it pays not to know what the future has in store. For that work, a strip of unstretched canvas six metres in length would end up being painted in a way that absorbed the last scraps of energy and health that remained mine to give away on the Gallipoli project. For now, I was painting the Tararua Mountains, and five boards stood blank in front of me. Were they an opportunity, or an accusation of having overreached my level of skill? Their stature was making me lie awake at nights. When I could so much do with the sleep, I spent hours wondering if I should go on.

It was time to start work. Selecting paints for such a large project was something I had not undertaken before. Guesswork was involved in quantity assessment. An order of large tubes had to be made so that I would have sufficient supplies on hand, not to be held up while the actual application of pigment was taking place. The tubes of titanium white, cerulean, Van Dyke brown, yellow ochre, raw and then burnt umber arrived. Burnt sienna and ultramarine would be mixed to make a vibrant black substitute. Violet added to darks would bring light to the painted surface, while sap green would take light away. These tubes and others gathered, filled with 120 ml or more, of pigment and promise. The moment of anticipation is one of the best—anxious and optimistic in equal parts.

Painting is an act of transformation through skill. So, one hot afternoon upstairs in the life drawing room, I sorted through tubes of paint, selecting raw umber to squeeze onto the pallet. The paint was thinned with turpentine, and I selected a scrubby, one-centimetre-wide, stiff-bristled brush with which I would sketch in outlines. Starting a painting is always a little bit of a threat to me, the person actually standing there with the brush. That act of applying pigment to the board or stretched canvas is sleight of hand, an alchemy forged often enough by imagination and chance. Skill helps, but the gifts of the best work arrive by knowing when to stop, or when to turn a mistaken brush stroke to advantage. My use of the Tararua Ranges in the Gallipoli exhibition seemed to be as much cheek and bullshit as any serious idea—or was it just accepting my roots?

My great uncle, Jack Dunn, grew up in the Wairarapa, and the exhibition was about him as well as Gallipoli.

127

Maybe he climbed up to Mount Holdsworth, looking north to the peaks whose image I painted close to ninety years after his death. Did he clamber that last grunt up the rocky face leaving the bushline below, breathing great gulps of cool air off the tops? What was it like for him, slogging up that other ridgeline to Chunuk Bair, with more bullets in the air than he'd made steps in a lifetime of walking towards this moment?

May 3rd
Am going to paint this on either 2 or 4 panels

looking north from
summit of Holdsworth
6.00pm 22 March 2003

Sometimes self-doubt struggles with our imagination in the tasks we set ourselves. We can take on too much information, and at other times not enough. Already a very old man and soon to die, Dad told me a little about his Uncle Jack. How Jack had carried him on his shoulders up the one hundred and thirty steps to Castlepoint lighthouse when it was opened late in 1913. Dad would have been five years old then, growing up in a world without aircraft, radio, tarsealed roads. My father did not even own a car until he retired, learning to drive in his fifties during 1963. Not one word was uttered about Anzac Cove in the few stories Dad told me of his childhood.

Tangential things can also happen while painting. The mind wanders, distractions appear over the horizon like spray off surf. The rhythm of the work invites the rash brush stroke. Other days, focus is total then suddenly a disoriented feeling arrives on a gust of late afternoon chill, or a car horn beeps, bringing you back from somewhere working with intense colour has taken you. It is almost as if I have to jettison all I know for a while, so that some work can be done. For now I just had to paint large lines, the thin mix of umber forming a skyline, roughly descending to where a ravine might tumble off a ridge, keeping it all loose and approximate. To get particular now would be to tighten up, to fight the process, and the finished work would show the fussiness. Somehow, the lines have to assert a freedom of purpose beyond my own levels of confidence, as if they know what it is that is beginning to happen before I do.

Raw umber, a worn-out brush, a painter with a story to tell and tentative lines placed on the left-hand board first. What am I doing? My idea is to use mountains that I look out to every day, from the porch of my home, to evoke thought about what happened at Gallipoli during July and August of 1915. Jack Dunn kept a journal in his time at Anzac Cove. The last entry was made on Wednesday 7 July. Records show he went back to hospital with dysentery. Before long, however, he discharged himself and returned to his post, still unwell but wanting to be with his mates.

He was placed on sentry duty, was not relieved at the posted time, and a couple of hours later was discovered by an officer asleep at his post. He was charged, and obviously he was guilty as charged. The court martial took place on 18 July, the same day as his commanding officer, Major Edward Cox, was able to write in his diary, 'Very quiet day, as usual hot and sultry. Fair amount of shelling but no fighting of any consequence in the trenches.' The unanimous verdict from the New Zealand officers in the court martial was a sentence of death. For three weeks, as a prisoner, Dunn sat in a shell crater under armed guard, knowing he was guilty but awaiting the sentence. It was not until 5 August that he learned of the judgement, as it had to be ratified by General Sir Ian Hamilton the Commander-in-Chief, who confirmed the sentence and remitted it.

Private J R Dunn's sentence was read to him, as he stood bare-headed in front of his regiment on 5 August 1915. Able to rejoin his unit, he was killed three days later on Chunuk Bair along with over 700 of his regiment.

The sentence, 'to suffer death by being shot', was duly read to the prisoner in front of his assembled regiment, and then the remittance awarded, due to previous good conduct and the health of the accused. By chance an Australian soldier standing up on the slope above the parade photographed the moment of the sentence being read.

He was the only New Zealander serving on Gallipoli to be sentenced to death in a Field Court Martial. The week before his offence, a New Zealand soldier from another unit, also found asleep on sentry duty at Anzac Cove, was given ten days hard labour.

In the research stage of my work about the Dunn family,

I drove out to Castlepoint to take part in a Founders' Day celebration in the little chapel overlooking the beach. A large wooden plaque is inscribed with the names of the settlers who were resident before 1875. Jack Dunn's Uncle John is buried in the cemetery there. His name is not inscribed, nor that of his sister who also settled there in 1875 and who went on to marry and prosper further north along the coast.

Talking to old Jock Perry, a local 'born and bred', that Founders' Day, I learned there was a bit of a scandal over Jack Dunn and his court martial sentence, back at Whakataki. Jock had no memory of the details as he was just a little nipper then. What he does remember is old Mathew Dunn giving a .303 rifle to his father about the time Mathew sold the farm, Willowbank, and moved into Masterton during 1921. Not long after that, in 1924 or 1925, Mathew's wife Sarah died of stomach cancer. She is buried in an unmarked grave in Masterton Cemetery. Mathew lost his marbles, and moved to Hampden to live with his daughter Agnes, my grandmother. By that time she was already a widow, hand-milking a few cows to earn a living while she raised five boys.

My grandmother, Jack Dunn's sister, kept a postcard depicting the burial truce one month after fighting started at Anzac Cove—when Turk and Anzac soldiers joined together in burying the dead in No Man's Land before returning to their trenches and recommencing hostilities. Flies, dysentery, rats, the smell of corpses that were lying decomposing between trenches which were only twenty metres apart in places—the imagination is unable to go there. The 24 May 1915 burial truce took place in that stretch of the trenches. Not one of her sons knew Gran White had that memento in the dresser beside her bed. I wonder which of her brothers, Jack or Mattie, sent her the card, as there is no message written on the reverse side of it. Perhaps she got it in some other way. She seldom left Hampden after the loss of her husband, and certainly never visited Gallipoli.

MAY. 24. 1915

I painted a panel for another Gallipoli series, and scratched in the surface pigment—

between the trenches
Turk swung shovel beside Anzac
from the sticks, swapped smokes
spoke in English to each other
we should all just bugger off home said one Digger
You go home, was the reply, I am home

More than one person who has been to Gallipoli mentioned to me how they thought, at first glance, the finished painting of the Tararuas was actually of Gallipoli. They thought I had seen the hills beyond Anzac Cove and painted an image of them. Most of the time, I was just trying to get the shadows right as they plunged down from the heights to swallow large chunks of the surface I was painting. The picturesque landscape of cerulean sky and fresh green grass or distant white-capped mountains does nothing to suggest the darkness that may await those who enter the mountains expecting a benign experience.

It was time to cover the glare of white gesso on which I had outlined the basic shapes I wanted to paint. There was underpainting to carry out, pale cerulean washes above the land, and large areas of shadow indicating the future presence of dark steep scree slides, or pale yellow ochre washes where tussock would later be indicated. Painting the Tararuas to represent the ranges inland from Anzac Cove resulted from a chance remark, read in a letter sent from the trenches at Gallipoli. An East Coast soldier told his mother that the hills of the Dardanelles Peninsula were just like the back of the farm; steep, covered in scrub. He chose not to mention the endless sniping, the lack of fresh water, or the presence of flies that clustered round food and rotting corpses alike. I can't remember if the letter features in Maurice Shadbolt's *Voices of Gallipoli*, or maybe it was in one of the diaries I read. There is such a mass of detail in researching a project like this Gallipoli story that the bulk threatens at times to develop a psychological whiplash capable of running away with the work, landing it just beyond reach for ever. Story after story contributed to a tentative understanding of what took place, but it was always limited, inaccessible in some way.

Empathy is insufficient to place me in the line of fire, or to put me in control of the trigger of a machine gun firing rounds into ranks of men running across flat lands three hundred metres away, or one hundred, or close enough to hear their screams, the thudding of their feet. Jack Dunn was a machine gunner on Quinn's Post during May and June of 1915.

In action for the first time on the day of the landings, men he had trained with were killed and wounded alongside him. During spells off the Vickers, Jack noted in his diary that he spent time sniping. In due course his brother Mattie also became a machine gunner, survived the war, and during the Second World War trained other men to fire weapons.

Perhaps the hills did remind the men of home, but they were a desperately long way from anywhere familiar. Thousands of soldiers, just like Jack Dunn, remain on the hills—or more accurately, as part of the hills. Many of their bones have been gathered and buried in communal graves, anonymous now as they were in 1915 when ill-advised commanding officers ordered them to their deaths. My father's Uncle Jack killed, and was killed, where wars have been fought for thousands of years.

In traditional oil painting, areas of shadow are painted early in the work. For a time the work takes on a sombre air, with large areas of black, near black or dark tones dominating the surface. I entered the mood of mountains forming before me, and could feel the chill rise from the valleys as evening closed over the room and I packed up each day. I had been working whenever the opportunity presented itself for some weeks now, and the shadowed forms started to take on definition, owning the space they occupied as I applied colour. The boards were a patchwork of Payne's grey, Van Dyke brown, dark violet, and my near black mix of burnt sienna and ultramarine, dark shapes overwhelming the initial, sketched, raw umber outlines. They anchored the landscape to the base of the boards. Painting Gallipoli in a studio on the other side of the world is hard work, but only in a relative sense.

During my youth, military training still took place for those whose birthdays were selected by ballot, to provide sufficient trainees for maintenance of a civilian territorial army. Around the time I was at Burnham Camp, in 1966, Prime Minister Keith Holyoake traded with the US government—beef quota in return for troops to serve in Vietnam. His fallback position, conscription, was never required as he obtained an export quota for New Zealand beef without going that far. Australia sent conscripts, in line with US policy. I appreciate not having had to fight in South East Asia, but would have if ordered to. At the time I was a farmhand on the West Coast, and did as I was told.

Strangely enough I spent time doing basic training as a machine gunner at Burnham. I managed to fire off a lot of blanks. It would be another thirty years before I learned of Jack and Matt Dunn, both machine gunners using live rounds at Gallipoli. It was with an eye for country as a potential machine gunner and my experience of tramping that I continued the painting in front of me. Mountains, a shaping of raw umber outline and sparse washes of colour subdued by big areas that would later depict shadow, began to be seen as moulded forms. The blend of greys, umbers and sienna, often mixed and rendered opaque with the introduction of white or yellow ochre, began to indicate rocks, ridges, slopes and faces in darkness, or catching light. The shadows retained their power.

Making the exhibition left me depleted in body and mind. The ten-year journey involved discovery of self as well, by turning the protective turf off the top of the past so that rain and wind could stir the mulch. In fact the very first painting pointing the way to Gallipoli was done years earlier as a present for Dad, long before the metaphorical dam burst open to show the bones of his uncle. Across from the old Whakataki pub was a cottage surrounded by macrocarpa trees. We walked through it and Dad told an anecdote, complete with embellishments, about climbing in the thickly branched trees while he once stayed there with his grandparents. So, being the son I was even at fifty, I dashed off a little water colour and presented it to him for Christmas.

During the year 2000, not long after Dad had died, I stood where his grandparents' house had once been more than remnant piles. A row of ancient stumps were reminders of macrocarpa trees that had once grown as a shelter belt. Between the Whakataki pub and the Tinui turn off, there is a place still known to old locals as 'Dunn's corner' and it is here that Jack Dunn (J.R.) was born, and where Dad's grandparents lived and worked their farm called Willowbank.

A few kilometres away, the place Dad so vividly recalled, belonged to another family's past, not ours. This episode as much as any other reminds me to be aware of the shadowed, often close to delusional nature of what I was doing, digging round, disturbing the past. Dad, the inveterate storyteller, could not be expected to remember accurately all the details back in that far off year when he was a little boy, but he could tell his stories with conviction and flair—and all the accuracy of a personal memory, recalled as a life lived.

I think of the apocryphal old man's axe, inherited by the eldest son. It has had two new blades and five handles over the years, yet now when another younger son owns it, it is still 'the old man's axe'. Dad had a way of taking a yarn and telling or retelling it, personalising it so that the details shifted to his own past. He could become the narrator, and revel in the vicarious experience. Yet, every so often over time, an outsider has authenticated one of his more outrageous exploits, recalled from a few wild youthful years, so that I am left with a legacy of shifting sand; bloody good yarns, few documented facts to go on, and someone who could always match anything we achieved as kids with a story capable of making our moment not quite what it was when we started telling the news. There were the stories of his time at Stillwater during 1926 or 1927, when he'd play cards all night, drinking and fighting, yet still go to work in the morning. One morning at Greymouth railway station in 1962, a retired guard came up to me.

'You look like Jack White's boy,' he said.

'That's right.'

He laughed. 'We used to call him the "tiger of the Coast" when he worked at Stillwater,' he said. 'One night he walked across the Grey River Bridge up on the guard rails. He was boozed—would've drowned if he'd fallen off.' Then he turned to wander off. 'Your father sure was a wild one.'

*

I'm glad Dad never learned that the house I painted in water colour, hung on his wall as a reminder of his childhood, was, to all intents and purposes, a fraud. That house he pointed out as the one where he'd visited his grandparents belonged to another family. His own was in a different site entirely. Oral history is full off traps for the unwary, it seems. At the time I painted that anonymous cottage I did not know Jack Dunn had ever existed. The environment of Dad's idyllic tree-climbing experience was to be dismembered soon after in real life. His parents shifted from Whareama to Hampden after his first year at school. And then the family struggled after his father's death in 1918. What he had for memories wasn't worth gifting to anybody in one sense, yet I still feel he could have shared more with his children as they grew up.

At a certain point in a painting, original sketches used to inform the process have to be put to one side. The work has a life of its own to be nurtured. It was time to give the pale cerulean sky mood and intensity equal to the ridgeline, with its imposition of rock, defying gravity to pierce cloud. I intended that skyline to be something that viewers would literally look up to, when the work was hung. Without any wish for the work to be romantic, I was fully able to sense the poetry of the dark range reaching into a pale blue sky, as if it were late afternoon—that time when shadows deepen, and if I am in the mountains, it is good to have already arrived at the hut, to be ready to put together a meal when the sunlight goes behind the western peaks.

While the past took on more than one intriguing layer, my next task was the layering of texture on the mountain forms with my brush or palette knife. The earlier applications of paint had dried sufficiently to work directly on top of them, an effect known as glazing. Here is the time to add richness to the colour, using layers of paint to create visual depth and intensity. What results is, I have to hope, rewarding to anyone who spends time looking at the work over any substantial

137

period. Subtlety and surprise will exist in the multiple layers of different colours or hues. Earlier pallet knife work had created stark effects, and now the glazing brush softened the surface in places, rendered it moody in others. *Tararuas as Gallipoli: Suite* was close to finished.

It was at this time that chance delivered a letter to me. In the book, *Letters from the Battlefield*, a soldier from Tinui, William Harvey, wrote to his parents and mentioned that he had seen Jack and Mattie Dunn who were both well. I went looking for William Harvey, and found his great-niece, Lorraine Kennedy, whom I had known for some time through library work. She turned out to be the custodian of the Harvey letters, and was happy to let me see them. On the afternoon of 31 January 2002, Catherine and I were sitting at the dining table, chatting with her about this and that. She took a dilapidated old biscuit box, and tipped letters onto the table, along with one or two photos and a live bullet from the Gallipoli campaign.

'Help yourself,' she said. Picking up one of the small folded pages covered in pencil writing she started reading. 'Oh. Listen to this.'

The first letter she had picked out of the little pile on the table was one sent to Willie's father on 1 April 1916. Trooper W. Nicholls is writing to Mr. Harvey of Whakataki about the battle in which his son Willie Harvey died of wounds.

Dear Mr Harvey,

Matt Dunn tells me that when I wrote to you from Alexandria, I did not mention the battle in which Willie was wounded & through which he lost his life. I'm very sorry indeed if I did not, but I believe I mentioned the date & in that case I'd probably not mention the name of the fight. Well, it was at Hill 60, and happened in the last week in August, I think the 27th. We have lately heard that one

138

of our fellows who was posted as missing since that date, is now reported to be a prisoner of war at Constantinople with two broken arms. Matty has only recently come back from England & all his correspondence has been accumulating at Abbassia (Cairo) Hospital. He got it yesterday & received something like fifty letters, including the one in which it said I omitted to mention the aforementioned battle . . .

It is terribly hot now & the flies are getting very troublesome & in a few months everything will be unbearable. The horses are all doing fine & want work badly. I was talking to a fellow from the Wellington Machine Gun Section who said he knew Jack Dunn & was near him when he was hit. Jack was shot through the [neck] throat, the bullet coming out somewhere in the back of the neck. Death was instantaneous. Jack Powell, Hankins, McDougal, Joe Donovan, Lofty, Nobby Clarke, Johnny Power, Jack Johnson, Matty & myself are all tip top & the only thing we all pray for is a trip to France & a cut at the Huns.

W. Nicholls
9th W.M.R.

p.s. Is Harry Lauder still at Awapiripiri or is he in camp as is rumoured here?

I phoned my sister Lesley. As a genealogist, I thought she might be interested in our find. When I told her of the letter and read its contents, she burst into tears. Later in the conversation, she told me she'd always wondered how Jack Dunn had died. The Chunuk Bair assault was vicious and fought at close quarters, and the wounded were stranded for hours unable to be carried off the side of the hill, without water or shade from the August sunlight. She had feared he was among those unfortunate men, many of whom suffered a lingering death from circumstantial neglect. The earlier letter mentioned by Nicholls, which was displayed in the exhibition, also informed the Cameron family of what happened to another Wairarapa soldier killed on Hill 60. Until they attended the exhibition opening they'd not known how their great-uncle died, or that he was the officer for whom Harvey served as batman.

The great dark shadows plunged off the steep sides of mountains dominating metres of painted surface, pushing the skyline into subservience to become a horizon forever just out of reach—just as the ridgeline of Chunuk Bair remained beyond the grasp of New Zealand troops the day Jack Dunn was shot. This painting was going to work. Now I just had to make sure I didn't fall at the last gasp.

Last minute highlights urged some rocks into prominence, some ridgelines forward, allowed others to fade. The painting was done. I was tired. This was the work that brought Jack Dunn as close to home as I would ever be able to bring him. All the painting, the writing, the exhibition space that were booked for Anzac Day 2005 was in memory of someone I had never met—and the content of the work turned out to contain truths for many others as well. At each showing of the work, various individuals have spoken to me, not about Jack Dunn, but about their great-uncle, grandfather or father who was lost to war.

Tararuas as Gallipoli: Suite had been finished with for nearly five years. It was Anzac Day. A group of us had decided on the spur of the moment to meet at our local war memorial plaque. Before dawn, I went with Catherine to join some friends down at the avenue of Memorial Oaks a couple of kilometres from here on Te Whiti Road. We walked in the dark through the thirty-six Memorial Oaks, while names were read, to where the cenotaph stands with those names inscribed. Those are the local men who went from this district during two wars, to fight and be killed. At the cenotaph, while candles burned in the half light, poppies and wreaths were laid, poems, including McCrae's *In Flanders Fields*, were read, a hymn sung, and a recording of the Last Post was played. A minute's silence was punctuated by the call of plovers. Ducks quacked as they flew off across the paddocks that surrounded us and somewhere magpies yodelled their chorus. As the dozen or so of us who had, on the spur of the moment, gathered, were now preparing to leave, the eastern sky bled red into colours of daylight. To the west standing silent and cobalt blue—the Tararuas, our horizon to this place, and sentinel to a small act of collective memory. Five years ago we weren't ready to hold a service here where we lived, even though a group of us usually attended a dawn parade at Masterton, or sometimes Martinborough or Tinui.

Later in the morning I drove out to Tinui, and went to the site of the first Anzac Day Service, where a cross was erected on 25 April 1916. On that day the cross bore seven names:

12/1532   **Bailey, H.**   Auckland Infantry Regiment
Died 25 April 1915
12/1533   **Leeming, G.**   Auckland Infantry Regiment
Died 25 April 1915
7/207   **Harding, W.F.** Trooper, Canterbury Mounted Rifles
Died 5 August 1915
4/811   **Langdon, H.L.** Sapper, N.Z. Engineers
Died 5 August 1915
10/84   **Dunn, J. R.**   Wellington Infantry Regiment
Died 8 August 1915
10/2494   **Robinson, R.** Wellington Infantry Regiment
Died 8 August 1915
11/290   **Harvey, J.W.B.** Trooper, Wellington Mounted Rifles
Died 2 September 1915

More names would have to be carved the following year, as the wooden cross formed the memorial for further casualties in Europe, as well as Gallipoli. With its silhouette against the skyline of the rocky Tinui-Taipo escarpment, the monument was a stark reminder of bodies that lay in soil far away from home.

Driving in a hurry, Catherine and I had reached Tinui in time to meet people who had taken part in their local service, and who were then having a cup of tea or coffee before heading home. We spoke with a few of them. Lorraine had poppies going to Gallipoli with a nephew who was travelling overseas. The poppies were to be laid beneath her great-uncle's name on Hill 60—Trooper Willie Harvey. Ian, Jock Perry's son, was able to tell me that he had now inherited old Matt Dunn's rifle, and that it is a family treasure. Paul and Rachel, who had seen *Tararuas as Gallipoli* at the Te Manawa exhibition on Anzac Day in 2008, said hello. They took part as students in a painting class I held in Auckland over twenty years ago. He attended Anzac Day in his RNZAF uniform.

There was much to talk about. We called in to the Tinui Museum and looked about. They are very aware that the centenary of their commemorative initiative will take place within six years. Their tiny building is due to become famous, it seems.

It was time to climb the 2.7 kilometre track to where the Cross is placed on the summit of the Tinui-Taipo rocks, 355 metres above the valley.

We did that. I walked alone. How it was for Jack Dunn's parents, I wondered. Did either of them attend the first memorial service? Did any of Mattie or Jack's brothers or sisters make the climb? At that time Mattie, the other son who served at Gallipoli, was still out there somewhere, in harm's way. It would be 1917 before they would see him arrive back, invalided home, a shadow of the man who had enlisted in 1914.

Despite the work of the exhibition, I am still unable to imagine Anzac Cove, Chunuk Bair, Hill 60 or Quinn's Post as battlefields. There are so many elements that make up the experience of trench warfare: the smell, constant sniping, the flies and illness, the fear of going to sleep and then of waking up, the loss of friends, the hallucinatory effect of idleness in a danger zone when the nerves scream for movement. How would I know? What would my response to that sort of experience have been? We are left with questions, words and questions. Neither words, nor my paint brush, are up to the task of providing answers.

When I finished painting *Tararuas as Gallipoli*, an allergic reaction to oil paints, turpentine and a raft of other chemicals hit me with debilitating power. After three decades of developing skills with the materials, I would no longer be able paint in oils. It has to be enough that I finished with my effort to honour the memory of Jack Dunn, and the others who died alongside him. At the moment the exhibition, *Gallipoli: In Search of a Family Story* lies in crates, stored in our garage, awaiting its next show, to be held in Waiouru Army Museum over Anzac Day 2010. It will be only five years from that exhibition of my work until the centenary of the Gallipoli landings.

It is just as well not one of us knows for sure what will turn up to be done as time passes. And no matter how hard we try, we are unable to know how it really is, or was, for someone else—mothers, brothers, uncles or great-uncles or total strangers. For most, what occurs is much less dramatic than the mayhem faced by men who ran across the beach at Anzac Cove on 25 April 1915. And how was it above the beach inland from Anzac Cove, during the following months of 1915? Those whose bones lie out there are the ones who know. Their mates who came home are all dead, and could not really find words to tell us anyway.

One woman who attended the opening of *Gallipoli: In Search of a Family Story* walked round the exhibition, taking a long time. All the while tears streamed down her cheeks. What was her story?

Beside the water

Over time our perspectives shift. Arriving in the Wairarapa gave me an opportunity to take in new information about what and where my family had been. Naturally enough that altered the balance of how I perceived the present. Some would say that being here changed me. Certainly there was a lot to take in, and both of us had to work at it. House building, working on and off the block for cash, there were daily pressures just as much as delving into family stories.

Every so often, Catherine would prevail upon me to get the hell out of the house and go fishing. I'd mooch along the banks of the Ruamahanga River on a summer evening, casting for trout where they rose to feed on insect hatches in the twilight warmth. There, without much success as a fisherman, I used time on my own to mull over the days, or the years. My older brother John died when he was fifty-four years old, only a couple of years after we arrived in the Wairarapa. I had visited his home in Upper Hutt once, and now mourned the lack of connection, even though we ended up living less than an hour's drive apart. Dad died in 1999, and with his death the last tie to the previous generation was gone. Mortality was in the air, along with memory. It was difficult to stand on the bank of a river without him entering my thoughts.

Dad was slightly mad about fishing. I reckon he could have happily fished with his line in a bucket of water out on the back doorstep most days. All my brothers and sisters were taken fishing, and sometimes he would have five or six of us in tow. It is hard to credit from this distance the dedication it must have taken to walk a few kilometres with children as young as four or five, then spend the day running after them, baiting hooks and throwing lines out. We even caught fish in those days, herring and flounder mostly. That is where fishing was best, down South Westland, at Ross. Hell, my sister Beryl even managed to catch herself one day, and Dad cut the hook out of her thumb with a razor blade. It was a long way to the doctor.

My earliest memories of going fishing with Dad were earlier than Ross though. He used to take me on the bar of his bike sometimes when he fished the Ashley River for trout. That was when we lived at Rangiora and I was five or six. I'd wander round the shingle river bed while he fished the evening rise for an hour or so. There was never much talk, but I learned to throw a stone that would skip across shallow water. Ross was after that time. We lived not far from the beach and the Totara River flowed behind the dunes before bursting through to the sea. One afternoon Dad shot a rabbit and then in the evening the men from the railway settlement went eeling. Using baling twine 'bobs' soaked in blood, with the rabbit trailing in the river, they caught eels that could have travelled many kilometres to the smell of the dead flesh. In torch and bonfire light, us kids played round on the bank, throwing eels back up the clay lip when they tried to slither back. One huge eel straightened out a stout steel gaff one of the men was using to hook other, what we thought were good-sized, eels out.

I hooked a trumpeter shark another night and when Dad caught up with me, I was being pulled toward the surf, still holding onto the line and calling out over my shoulder.

'I think I've got a big one Dad.'

We used to eat a lot of fish in those days. Dad also went out by himself a lot. He could arrive home ready to fillet what would be cooked for the next couple of days.

After Ross we moved to New Plymouth. Fishing stopped as there were no rivers close enough for us kids to go with Dad. A year or two later at Maungaturoto it was just as bad. Once or twice friends took Dad out in their boats, fishing for snapper on Kaipara Harbour, but that was it, apart from a few mud eels in farm creeks.

Our next shift was to Rotorua. It is strange to think that about fifty years ago I used to go trout fishing in the middle of what is now suburban housing and sealed roads. The Utahina stream gurgled and twisted through farmland within biking distance of Clinkard Avenue where we lived. Saving my paper-round money I bought a split-cane trout rod and reel for about four pound ten when I was probably not quite twelve. Dad and I used to bike out to the paddocks and wander the Utahina for hours. I'm not sure why my younger brothers never went then, as a few years later in Greymouth they were often out with Dad, especially after I left home. My older brother John and Dad never got on and fishing seldom seemed an option. To be honest, I got sick of him saying all the time, 'I've got a bite!' all excited, then when everyone was looking, 'Oh, I think I've lost it.' Fishing is a quiet business.

With that little split-cane rod I caught my first trout. Dad often told the story afterwards about how I offered him flies I had learned to tie at the tackle shop on Tutanekai Street. He decided to go for lures he bought from the shop. My clumpy imitations of a *Parson's glory* meantime incited two trout to attack my line that day. I reeled them in. Dad caught nothing. We'd talk about which flies or lures to use often after that, although he seldom used anything I tied. His preference lay with those he read about in his outdoor magazines: *Blue*

Dun, Greenwell's Glory, Black Gnat, Hair and Copper, Pheasant Tail, tiny works of art and deception that mixed feathers and fabric, wool and wire.

By the time we moved to Greymouth at the end of my third-form year, fishing was as natural as breathing. I knew as much about casting for trout as I did about bowling a cricket ball or scrapping with my older brother. Fishing was synonymous with being in trouble for arriving home late. When kahawai were running we'd take our thread-line gear down close to the river mouth. In the whitebait season we were out there with our nets.

For all that, if I think about fishing now the first thing to come to mind is a river bank at night. Darkness before the moon has risen, and stars low over the trees crowding the opposite bank. There are sounds: a ripple of current tugging at branches a few yards away, somewhere a lazy flop of a big trout breaking the water after a moth, maybe an inquisitive cow munching her cud. Somewhere downstream the glow of a cigarette tip and that will be Dad, line out, waiting in silence. From time to time a cough will break the peace. He knew the day would come when he'd have to chuck in smoking.

When we were at Ross, Dad would tie nylon knots, bait hooks, cast handlines and sinkers out into the lagoon or over the waves. By the time I left home, his bi-focals were letting him down. I'd not stray too far, especially if I was carrying the torch. It was important to listen for the sounds of waders splashing to the bank.

'You right, Dad?' I'd call into the darkness.

'Another bloody snag,' he'd call back. 'Lost the god damned lot.'

'I'm on my way.' Moments later I'd have the torch out, and gather elusive nylon fishing line that he was unable to see, and too arthritic to hold when he could see it. A few well-practised movements he'd taught me years earlier and

147

with a newly attached fly in the water, Dad would be back where the meaning of life held clarity, holding a rod waiting for a hungry trout to strike. Maybe tonight would be a good one, and we'd smell of fish guts and have scales sticking to the bottom of our tackle bags before we got home, inevitably late, always regretful at breaking the spell.

I'm glad Dad never revisited Rotorua and saw the muddy little drain the Utahina has become. He doesn't know that the Hinds River, where I poached many a succulent breakfast of trout, and where he joined the fishing while on visits to my own young family, is now a dry creek bed, all the water siphoned off for irrigation up stream. Dad doesn't need to know about the foreshore and seabed debate. His stories have been lived, told, and are safe with his memory.

He'd be disappointed to know that the weather has been so bad this season that I've only managed to get out once to fish the Ruamahanga River that flows just five minutes' drive from my home. Yet in some ways that would be the least of issues for him to deal with. Would his world have been able to even begin comprehension of the arrival of didymo, or rock snot as his disgusted voice would have described it, in our rivers? The rivers first to be affected, those in Southland, were his favourite fishing place in the world. Being the man he was, I suspect Dad would have taken the pestilence of didymo as a personal affront.

When a report arrived recently suggesting that the Ruamahanga is highly polluted, he would have spent hours lamenting change when he visited me, just as likely harking back to the river he fished with his brother Allan the last day they spent together, in the back country behind Wanganui. He described fishing a crystal-clear pool where deep water swirled down near rock and roots of ancient trees. Using cicada lures sucked deep into the current they caught trout with ease. But it was the water that excited him, the quality of clarity over stone in the sunlight. At another spot that day, their companion stepped into water that looked to be a couple of feet deep, and went in up to his chest. His brother Allan died of a heart attack only weeks later. He was only 48 years old. Dad never went back to that river—unless you count the times he told the story of that last day with his brother.

His next visit to my local river, and the sight of effluent bubbles of unknown provenance floating downstream, would have him expressing further disgust. Reeling in a line covered in green slime and removing the stuff before another cast would just as likely have provoked lurid expletives about irrigation depleting water flows and heating the river each summer. God alone knows what his reaction to algal bloom would have been. To be made to stay away from the river each summer, awaiting cooler temperatures, would have caused irritation that just had to be spread around, being too much for one soul to cope with.

'Change is not a bad thing.' I can hear echoes of his voice. 'But what the hell is going on?' To have waterways where perfectly fit dogs could die just from swimming or playing in them, as they can when algal bloom is rife, he would think an utter scandal by the gods of fair play.

If I were a young man with children now, living in the country as he once was, it is inconceivable that on a Saturday morning or a quiet summer evening I'd put one of them on the bar of my bike and trundle off to the local river for an hour or two fishing. Not where I live now anyway. Competition is high on the road, and fishermen are up and down the bank like a rash. Seasonal depletion of water flow through irrigation for dairy farming ensures that trout are few and far between, and certainly they are fly shy through constant disturbance. If one is serious about fishing, then it is a matter of more substantial travel, and that means getting in the car.

And it isn't only about fishing. Dad made connections. To

149

him the equation would have been extremely simple: healthy trout equal healthy waterways which in turn equal healthy environments. I said earlier that it is now over fifty years ago that we fished the Utahina stream as it meandered round the outskirts of Rotorua, over land long since smothered by housing. At that time, tourism was a comparatively benign industry, but sometimes Dad would gather any of us boys who were around and head off on bikes toward Ngongotaha to visit Rainbow Springs, or a bit further out to Fairy Springs. These were a couple of places where tourists could see trout in those days. Precise detail is a bit hazy but in general terms I think the Rainbow Springs trout were more confined in some way. Some of them had growths on their jaws, or other abnormalities as I remember it. What I do remember clearly, is Dad talking then about pollution of water by fertiliser, timber treatment and industrial waste. To be talking like that in the 1950s is, when I think about it now, remarkable. Dad had shifted round a lot, and seen a lot of waterways. He probably knew quite a bit that was seldom expressed, but he'd spent more hours looking at water by then than most of us would in a lifetime.

Of course I was only about twelve, and all that worried me about rivers was fishing. I'd often go into that shop selling fishing gear on Tutanekai Street. That was where the owner, sensing my enthusiasm, very generously taught me to tie trout flies, and where I bought my first trout rod. These days, I'm thinking more of Dad's concerns about water. By looking back it is possible for us to position where we are now, by way of contrast, which is not a comfortable exercise. So much for progress is all I can say. It may not only be the trout whose future is in jeopardy from the way we use and abuse our waterways.

People like my old man knew that the wild world had to be looked after. His magazines, *Field & Stream*, *National Geographic* and *Forest & Bird,* were always lying around the place. He perceived that an economy that measured success in terms of monetary gain turned its back on what a close observation of the natural world could teach us, which is that our health depends on the health of a whole lot of other creatures. I think he also understood that it is the task of each generation to demonstrate values to the next, what it means to care.

All those hours with the fishing line in the water. I've come round to thinking, it isn't about catching fish. Dad was teaching me the value of pausing a moment, of being part of something natural. Thing is, he taught me without saying a single word about it.

By walking

The duck left the water of the dam and safety. Followed by three ducklings she started up the slope across the rough ground of the overgrown bank. Head held high, pausing frequently, she looked about on full alert as she moved away. The ducklings, not yet ten days old, waddled comically over, round and through the rushes and coarse grass that towered over them. Past the fence and into the paddock the little group scurried. Out there where visibility was high, they encapsulated the term, sitting ducks. They were travelling directly over the same ground that three or four wandering cats used to scavenge on our place. Who the cats belonged to is anyone's guess. They have been out and about most days in recent weeks. If the timing of the ducks proved to be unfortunate, some cat will have fed on duckling before the morning ended. The duck kept up a constant twittering to the ducklings' running, trying to keep them in a group, while they made forward progress in short random bursts that seemed always a little chaotic.

Three days ago this clutch of ducklings was heading along the gully away from the dam at the same time as one of the cats prowled over the paddock towards the bridge under which they would pass. While we watched, the situation developed into one of inevitable catastrophe. But for once, chance intervened. A harrier hawk, during its seemingly ceaseless patrol for prey, drifted over the gully without spotting the family of ducks. Instead, down over the cat the dark wings swept, and the tabby took off for the dense thicket of Tasmanian Blackwood trees the other side of the paddock. For the time being the duck and her ducklings were safe.

When it comes to walking over open ground the contest between ducklings and predator is clearly unequal. The hawk can fly, the cat can run, and both are equipped with deadly weaponry to tear the life out of vulnerable smaller creatures. Ducklings may evoke laughter and delight with their antics, but before they are able to fly, and until their size prevents predators attacking them on the water, ducklings are really easy prey. Any chance of survival depends on their habit of scattering when they run. Their lives depend on it. What we see as comical, and what drives the duck dotty as she attempts to maintain a semblance of togetherness in her brood, also ensures that predators are able to chase only one at a time. If the tiny ducklings stayed together their enemies would feast on the lot. As it is they can only pick them off individually. An instinct to scatter provides for the sacrifice of one life in order to buy time during which surviving ducklings will grow. In the days when we had a cat, more than once over a period of days, a brood of ducklings would be seen to fade from ten or eleven, to nine, eight . . . until the entire brood was gone. Our cat would put on weight each spring, on a rich diet of wildfowl and other fledglings.

Why ducklings have to travel overland from dam to dam each spring is beyond my understanding. Does the constant movement make them elusive in some way? Perhaps they are genetically wired to move about wetlands, and human activity such as draining swamps, grazing grass with sheep and generally disrupting their watery habitat renders them vulnerable in new ways.

*

153

Many thousands of years ago, perhaps a similar situation existed for the first human groups venturing out from the shelter of the forest canopy into the savannahs beyond, where there was abundant food, but also danger. Being able to walk or run was no protection in the presence of predators possessing speed, flight, fangs or talons, but humans adapted and developed other abilities to enable them to defend their group. An upright posture enabled our human predecessors to see predators, as well as food, more easily. The ability to walk upright was also probably a major contribution to human beings being able to colonise all corners of the earth. Our contemporary society seldom leaves us vulnerable to predation in the way the ducklings out on our paddocks are today. There is still something disturbing about too much comfort that makes many of us become trampers, pilgrims, or otherwise to use our ability to walk in order to challenge our physical resources in wild places.

Catherine talks of walking somewhere, alone. Not without people necessarily, but without anyone she knows, in a place she has not been before. She goes walking every day.

'Walking,' she says. 'It is a moment of joy.'

There are times the walk is only in her mind, a world of imagination and longing. More often, with boots on, she will set out. As I watch her figure moving down the shingle drive, there is a sense of life being as it should be. Wind may be blowing, sun might shine, frost may linger, yet the sound of her feet, fading out of reach on the stones, suggests all is well. Minutes later, from where I sit at my desk, she can be seen walking northward toward the oak trees, pausing on the road verge as a car passes, then regaining her stride moments later.

Sometimes she carries a recorder and microphone, capturing sound along the way. When the recordings are played in different surroundings, such as an art installation space, possibly with selected objects placed in it, they can alter the space. The sound can be reproduced in a variety of ways using technology. Such sound-saturated productions become sound sculpture which responds to architectural space. Sound has the ability to evoke all sorts of different reactions from people who listen within the given space.

Her sound works record the rhythm of her walking steps against surfaces; bitumen, shingle, the grass verge, a steady cadence designed for distance. All around there are other sounds as well: birds, sheep and cattle, dogs, vehicles and sometimes people. Several recordings have been made of the hour it takes to walk to the Memorial Oaks and back. Each sound work possesses personality, particular to the day on which it was recorded, often distinct from others only through subtle detail.

In the avenue of oaks planted about sixty years ago the air is different, often cool on a hot summer's day, or quiet beneath the canopy when a nor'wester is all bustle across the paddocks and whipping ripple effects on the surface of the Taueru Creek that runs to the south side of the oak plantings. One oak tree planted for each man from the local district killed during the First and Second World Wars—to form an avenue where the Carterton and Masterton District Council boundary lies. The men grew up on farms, or in little settlements: Te Whiti, Longbush, Gladstone or the Admiral, perhaps out toward Te Wharau. Not far from the trees is a plain cenotaph, similar to many like it throughout the country, with names inscribed in concrete. Where the road passes between the trees, if there is a break in passing traffic, something happens—nothing mystical, but a sense of peace or seclusion filters into the place. There, Catherine records the sound of birds, or cars bursting past doing more than a hundred kph. She would like to see the oaks treated with a touch more respect. If people walked that stretch of road instead of going past encapsulated in speed machines, she believes, they would treat the area differently.

Walking is part of a sense of place. There is an old farmer's saying: 'The land isn't yours until you have travelled the boundary on foot.' The very idea of a walking around a farm on foot is now a fanciful notion. In this age of the ATV (all terrain vehicle), or farm bike, where farms are amalgamated for economies of scale, and large acreages are often leased well away from home, farmers seldom walk more than is absolutely necessary. They haven't got time between dawn and dusk. The accountant has hijacked the notion of belonging. Half the time he is part of a consortium that owns the bloody farm, if the banks don't own it by mortgage.

For years we walked on farmland, over hills behind our place rather than along the road. When the farm was sold we asked the new owner if it was okay to continue to do so.

'No,' he said.

It was time to look elsewhere to walk.

This week we've been walking at Morere, through bush very different from the kind that we find growing in the Wairarapa. Here, further north, vegetation is comparatively lush, growing without the hard frosts or snowfalls that assault our hills each winter. Nikau palms and kawakawa grow abundantly, along with other dense foliage. The same bird species inhabit this area, though in greater numbers. During one walk we visited the local cemetery, a clearing tucked in the bush, hedged with blackberry and bracken. In neatly mown grass, headstones stood in tidy rows, one or two with plastic flowers placed in front of them. The most recent burial, Esther, was born in 1908, the same year as my father. She lived in the district until 2000, when she was buried in a plot looking out to the hills. According to the headstone her father died in 1918. She lost her father at the same age as my Dad, who also lived until he was in his nineties. And, I wonder, did Esther's father also die during the Spanish flu epidemic? Random connections like this draw my eye. Perhaps particulars of the object single it out from others around it.

Back on the bush track we continued walking, keeping an eye open for tui, kereru and tomtits as they flitted or flew through the canopy. My friend Paul Martinson has painted birds for decades, simply because he is fascinated by their ability to occupy air space among the trees, which is something that is beyond our natural capacity. At one point a fantail flew close enough to touch the shirt I was carrying. Back and forth it darted, hoping perhaps that I'd brush the cloth against track-side foliage, disturbing some insects upon which it could feed. Catherine also carried the recorder on that walk. Back home in our living room we will be able to listen to the bell-like voice of tui, beat of kereru wings in flight . . . birdsong captured clear as a back-porch wind-chime.

Walking locates us, defining our limitations within physical boundaries. What distance can be covered in a day's walking? Or trudged in a week? Many factors affect the final reading of where we belong. Maori might express it as turangawaewae—a place for the individual to stand, deeply rooted within a genealogy offering spiritual connection to the land. That is a concept for the people of the land—tangata whenua. It is too late for post-colonial Pakeha to return to their Celtic (or other) roots, after several generations of being settlers in this land. Is it too soon to claim the right to be of this place? Born here, we'll likely die here. Our children have been born here. A story of place, as a shared story, is developing in these islands of Aotearoa/New Zealand.

'You see,' Ka, who grew up at Whakarewarewa, told me, 'the old kuia believed that walking around in bare feet allowed your body to touch the earth, to be with our whenua.'

To have mud or sand against our skin, or sliding between our toes, is as close as we can come to the physicality of a place, to connect with the earth we stand on. Ka might say we can become part of the earth's breath, with our bare

157

feet in the dirt. Without touching the earth, we do not truly know the place on which we stand. Place is more than a story of people and events, the past preserved in our minds; it is also sensory, to be felt through the feet and hands as much as seen through the eyes.

I go out walking in this place, and there are familiar visitations: wind blowing over the mountains bringing a taste of the Tasman Sea, rain dropping by on a visit from the Pacific Ocean, migratory birds proclaiming this moment to be their time, and not least, the sun and moon, easing in and out of their seasonal variations. There is no morning exactly the same as yesterday to wake to. The 'place' is never quite the same place, but it is where I am, a place to be.

Over the last summer Catherine wrote a thesis to provide a theoretical basis for her art practice. So many hours she spent looking for artists whose work reflected the walking/ sound recording aspect in her work. Some, like Janet Cardiff, came close with recordings of walking activity, but there was no one right there. She was walking that pathway alone it seemed. Alone until last week that is. Heading north for our holiday, and in no hurry, we stopped to walk by the shops at Woodville. There was a second-hand bookshop. What the hell, we were on holiday and bookshops are always a temptation. Now, to be honest Woodville is not the centre of art theory or practice, yet I bought a book titled *Notes on the Unpainted Landscape*, a catalogue for a Scottish exhibition, dating from 1986. Since recently reading Kathleen Jamie's essay collection, *Findings*, I've been on a bit of a Scotland trip in my imaginings. I've an unrealised desire to go walking in Scotland, especially where my ancestors may well have walked. Of course, it was too late to help in Catherine's thesis writing, but on page ten I found this:

David Tremlett opened up his tape-recorder on a journey in 1972 in each of the old counties: Murrayshire, Morayshire,

Westmoreland, etc. The random sound of *The Spring recordings* becomes its own pastoral, of birdsong, of wind, of movement in the landscape. The work is presented as a shelf of eighty-one tapes, each one lasting thirty minutes. It sits as a silent wall work, referring to its source and its potential replay.

Even walking into a second-hand bookshop can have its rewarding aspects, and to find a book that supplied a precedent to her practice excited Catherine. She is attached to the idea that sounds are of a place, and as particular as the tactile and visual markers we usually use as identities. When she walks, she hears a place as much as she sees it.

She would say that walking takes us into an immediate reality, using more senses than sight, and making us listen to sound that is unedited. Our engagement with our surroundings becomes more intimate. Looking at, and listening to, the leaf fall of autumn as I walk round our place allows a memory to surface that is spectacularly present, yet also somehow slightly vague.

It is clear and sunlit, yet the sun shines on a heavy frost where shadows have delayed the morning thaw. I am walking to school, so we must be in Rangiora. I don't know how I happen to be walking alone. Surely I would normally have gone to school with my older brother and sisters. Trees that have big round trunks with smooth strong bark stand either side of the pathway down which I walk. Did we walk through a park to school at Rangiora? This morning is so light and crisp. I kick at heaps of fallen leaves, then run and kick, and feel leaves push up round my shoes onto my legs, hear them rustling, smell the dryness of them. They are lying so thick on the ground. I jump and hop, make dry crunchy leaves fly high in the air.

Is this the place where I learned to play conkers with horse chestnuts, and where I learned to make a helicopter with a pin and sycamore seedpods? I don't know. There are so many places to be remembered. What I am able to take from the memory of that morning is how I was part of something, the autumn world fully alive. I like the American term for autumn, *fall*, with its soundings of ripe fruit, harvesting and leaves turning to enriched hues, sufficient to give a colourist memorable dreams.

In an even earlier time I am walking through leaves also, up a pathway at Granity, with Granddad Kirkwood. This memory is more tenuous. Trees overhang and provide shade for moss to grow over what may have been concrete or brick, I can't recall. It is nice to be walking beside this man, who wears an old suit coat and smokes a pipe. He is able to chuckle over something, and I feel safe. I was staying with him and Grandma Kirkwood, of whom I have no memory at all. The memory of my mother's father may be the first memory I have.

Above my desk is a photo of Grandad and me, taken in 1969, and that is the last time I stayed with him. He is filling his pipe. I am twenty-five, just about a head taller than him, and skinny as a rake, recovering from the viral meningitis that meant giving up the lease of a dairy farm at Blackwater. We are both concentrating on his pipe-filling, heads bowed in the sunlight. Even now his shoulders are broad, his stance upright. There is no evidence that decades of work as a bushman, miner and farmer buffeted him one little bit. He is eighty-one years old, and his name, which I have inherited, was Valdimir. We have no record of how that particular Christian name appeared in the family, but there is plenty more we do not know as well. Only a few stories were told relating to Val Kirkwood. Prone from time to time to arrive home late at night after walking from the Granity pub, singing the songs of the happy drinker, he lived pretty much under the thumb of his wife, or so the story goes, but there were occasional moments when he asserted himself, showing his wild Irish roots.

Recently I read that Seamus Heaney grew up and went to school with Kirkwoods at Anahorish, which is not far from Enniskillen where my own ancestors lived in Ireland before emigration to Australia. I can't help wondering what it is like to grow up where families of the same name have dwelt for generations, to be connected to a place in that way. Where language is local, and history shared by neighbourhoods of people who know each other inside out. What sort of certainty does that give a writer's voice?

That sort of belonging owns a dark side of course. Our own family stories highlight one aspect of the locality in which Heaney spent his childhood. It seems that when the Enniskillen mob came out to New Zealand, they brought a little bit of the sectarian Paddy in their veins. My grandfather, that extremely mild man by all accounts, chased a priest off his farm with an axe one day. Apparently the priest wanted

Val Kirkwood, second from right, during railway building north of Westport. Late in 1920s.

to negotiate a deal with Granddad, as father of the girl one of his flock members wished to marry. Mum inherited her father's sectarian prejudice and, as karma works in cack-handed ways, she was rewarded by three of her sons marrying Roman Catholic girls. On the day of my older brother's wedding, I sat in the back of the church alone. No other members of my family turned up to hear his vows, or to hear the soloist sing an *Ave Maria*. After the service I walked home through the streets of Greymouth, alone, and not for the first time, enjoying the solitude that walking places could give me.

There is another story about my grandfather. As a boy, he crossed the Southern Alps, walking with his father, to settle north of Westport. Their horse carried essential tools, a sack of flour and a side of bacon. For a large part of my life I carried scraps of memories including this one of Granddad walking through the mountains as a boy. I would take them out, polishing them to look at the way they shone, in what seemed my own scrambled existence, my reality in shades of grey.

There is a Roman saying which I read first in *Nature Cure* by Richard Mabey, '*solvitur ambulando*'—you can work it out by walking. Catherine and I have done a lot of walking and tramping, and often a lot of talking while we walked. Among the beech trees, or along the river banks, we have sought out common ground with quiet chat, and at times entered stony silences in which only walking has allowed us to occupy the same space. With a need to get to the next hut, and spend the next three days together before the tramp is finished, walking is a certain way of learning how to get on with each other. Putting up with each other's little ways is an ongoing adjustment each morning, just as our boots need to be laced up, or the activity of tramping is intolerable. Mostly the wisdom of the Roman stands true: walking solves problems, just as activity of any sort is often the best medicine.

Sometimes our words have conveyed uncertainty of how to act toward each other. Then we are like those ducklings I watched between stretches of water, on our way into the unknown. In fact, next time I saw the little brood, two ducklings were through the fence in the paddock, but the duck kept stopping to look back, until at last the third duckling appeared. They set off, but again the duck stopped and turned. Duckling number three was not keeping up because, for whatever reason, it appeared to be lame. A tailend Charlie, it hopped about, vulnerable while it paused a moment to catch its breath, and then raced after the others. I watched the slow progress across the grazed grass, until at last, without the appearance of cats or hawks the duck ushered her brood through the fence into long rubbishy growth and comparative safety.

Nothing like the visceral danger of the ducklings' forays exists for Catherine and me when we are out walking. Often enough there have been moments of well-being for us, out tramping, when the day has been long and at last the hut appears fifty metres along the track, through the trees. Up the Travers Valley, or going toward Totara Flats, or Sunset Saddle, there is a quiet satisfaction to be had from taking a pack from your shoulders and pushing the hut door open after a strenuous walk. At other times, the feeling of arrival might verge on elation if the weather has packed up, and we have been carrying packs in country that is demanding. When wind and sleet are driving across the track to the Angelus hut, in the Nelson Lakes region, spectacular views become a grey blur of hostility. The simple thought of dry gear and a burning fire on those days can be what keeps tired legs going.

The mountains are not easy, however, and danger can turn up suddenly for the unwary or ill-prepared. A young friend and I went deerstalking in the Taipo Valley on the West Coast, a comfortable overnight jaunt from Hokitika.

Waking to heavy rain we had a quick bite to eat and a hot drink before clearing off. When we reached the bank, it was still possible to see the bed of the Taipo River, so we crossed safely enough, even though we got a dunking. With a two-to-three-hour walk out to the road, there should have been no drama, except that our effort coincided with a monumental cloudburst over the watershed of the Taipo catchment. The track that was well known to us became another creature, a water dragon flowing and gushing from unlikely sidings, a sinuous snake of current, pulling at our boots on muddy inclines. More than once walking through the trees we tripped or stumbled on unseen obstacles, tree roots or ruts. Clothing became heavy from saturation, and the noise of rain was only obliterated by the roar of the river where the track sidled along the bank above it. Then we heard the rocks of the riverbed start to roll, an uncontrolled bassline beneath the incessant beating of rain against wet weather gear, trees and earth. The rumbling growl seemed to grow out of the mud we walked through, a vibration we felt rather than heard. There was nothing to do but walk on. In due course, we reached the end of the bush track, and ahead of us were open flats, rocky and rough, the result of past floods, avalanches, earthquakes and slips.

It stopped raining. The wind blew harder, and all round us the sound of running water reminded us of the past two hours. By now we were cold and getting colder, without the windbreak provided by the bush. We needed to push on. There would be a car waiting for us just over half an hour away where the track ended. Water continued to pour off the hills, and over the stony country small runnels now surged in frothing narrow channels only inches deep, but rapid and treacherous. Even something a couple of metres wide had to be treated with respect. Narrow channels could be jumped—but the landing was far from safe as cold feet clumsily scrambled among rock. Our chilled bodies would easily make a false stride and twist an ankle. Slowly we progressed, slowly the going got easier, until we reached a rampant sluice just a little wider and a little steeper than the others.

Bracing tentatively, I edged into the white water, and then Lewis crossed, using my rifle and braced body for support. That is how narrow this water barrier was. He could get across in two strides from where I stood. On the other side he took off his pack and stood ready to reach out and help. I turned slightly, arms spread wide for balance, my legs almost numb with cold, fumbling for solid bottom. Rocks moved beneath my feet. Down I went. Everything was noise, water and noise. I hit something big and solid—a rock, a tree trunk—and it turned me. Right way up, I scrambled onto the other side through rocks that scraped skin and rolled as I grabbed at them, and at the water fluming toward the Taipo in full flood thirty metres away down the slope.

'Fuck!' I staggered upright.

'You okay?' Lewis ran towards me. 'Jesus!' He couldn't believe it. 'Y'okay? It happened so fast!'

And we started to laugh. This wasn't glad to be alive—this was slightly manic, a touch hysterical. Then we stopped. I was alive. The wind was blowing. I was chilled to shaking.

'Yeah,' I stepped carefully toward the track. One leg throbbed, and there was blood and water running off my hand. 'Yeah, I think so. Let's get the hell out of here.' It was too cold to check what was what. Everything worked. I wanted to make sure we made it to that vehicle. In a few minutes we passed off the rock faces onto rough pasture, walking through small pockets of bush from time to time, back to the road. Gentle rain started to fall as we walked the last 50 metres, before getting into the waiting van and travelling back to town.

The Roman sage of *solvitur ambulando* would suggest, perhaps, that unless the raw-edged elements are faced, the delight in comfort fades and becomes commonplace. Were the thoughts of this Roman perhaps penned safely inside, away from rough weather or dangerous terrain? Whenever I have been in a position of danger, I am too bloody busy, uncomfortable or just plain scared, to suggest that anything can be worked out by walking.

'What the hell are you doing here, you silly bastard?' I am more likely to be thinking to myself.

Yet, to be outside and walking is one of the easiest ways to face the world without too many intermediary safety nets. It is being physically honest. Good boots and decent clothing are all that is needed. There is indeed something elemental in the satisfaction felt in taking boots off aching wet feet, after hours in the bush, or on rock above the bushline. It is also invariably pretty bloody good to get back to a comfortable bed and a good feed.

Before long, however, the idea of walking in the mountains returns. To live as we do here, in sight of peaks and ridgelines, is a reminder of what it can be to walk away from roads, away from comfort. Any danger that exists tends to be there by our own choice, as we are happy enough to titillate our senses a little, to feel a tinge of apprehension in a creek crossing, or the negotiation of a scree slide, where balance is everything between safety and a skin-scraping fall. To spend time out in the open has been an option sought after by many people, especially since populations started to congregate and live in cities. There is a whole raft of literature in which authors such as Wordsworth—'I wandered lonely as a cloud'—praise time spent walking. Philosophers, such as Nietzsche, walked every day by choice. Kant and Burke confronted the philosophical questions of the 'sublime'— that when faced with the power of nature in true wilderness, it took the observer beyond the ability of words to express the feelings the experience evoked. I'll settle for taking off wet socks, lighting a fire and getting into a warm sleeping bag as being something sublime, when the Gods of Nature rage in wild places. I have no desire to climb Mount Everest. To be above the bushline in Nelson Lakes, or on the Tararua tops across the valley, is enough for me.

There are things I would like to do, however, and places I'd like to go. I'd like to smell and touch the earth of Islay, the Hebridean island my mother's Kirkwood forebears started out from, and walk round Lanarkshire out of Glasgow where the Dunn family is first recorded. The idea of going for a long walk is also tantalising. To get up day after day and walk, in the manner of pilgrims, would be an experience worth having. Human beings have always trekked, travelling with hope in search of a sense of belonging, walking towards the horizon. I do not need a sacred site to wonder what is beyond a rise in the terrain, all I need is to go and look. One of the things that Catherine and I have spent time talking about when we've got packs on our backs, and the pathway recedes into the distance, is how good it would be to spend weeks walking somewhere, just for the hell of it. If that is what we want to do, then we'd better get on with it.

It is time to plan on doing more than talk about walking somewhere. It is time to put on boots and step out, before old age means we can't bend down and lace them up. This morning, rain is falling steadily. I have found myself looking toward the dam where the surface reflects the sullen grey cloud, and the dark colours of sodden vegetation. A couple of mallard drakes fly in, only to be disturbed and fly off again. They set up a racket, and quack exasperation for the entire neighbourhood to hear. Speckled light is the pattern of each raindrop hitting the dam surface, causing a hypnotic and constant movement. There are no ducklings today.

Andy dropped by to fell a couple of trees with his chainsaw. My own saw is too small to handle the large radiata pine we have decided will do for next winter's firewood. The noise of his work will keep any birdlife wary and distant.

'I saw a couple of paradise ducks yesterday,' he told me when I mentioned our lack of ducklings in the brood. 'They had one duckling.' He laughed with characteristic good humour. 'Hey, what's going on? I just about had a word with them. They always have a dozen or so in tow. This pair was being lazy.'

'We've got a load of wild cats around,' I suggested.

'Yeah,' he answered. 'It's been a soft winter. Maybe more predators have survived than usual?'

'Bloody things—'

'Y'know,' he went on, 'I've heard of hawks landing on ducklings and using their weight to hold them under and drown them.'

'Christ!' I looked down at my boots, time to lace them up, then go and attend to the trees.

As we walked over the paddock I wondered how the lame duckling is managing. Is he still there, keeping out of sight? Over the next few days, if the duck arrives back, we'll learn what has gone on, more or less. The fact is, we'll probably never know for sure. She'll either have ducklings with her, or she won't. It will work out, as the Roman says, but we are unable to guarantee what result is over the horizon. When our body takes us walking, who knows what will happen in the mind. Walking into unknown territory is hazardous.

Lie of the land

Harrier hawks patrol our land as if it is theirs. They use the spread of their wings to glide over dams and olive groves with habitual shyness, veering away if we happen to be outside and moving about. Across the road, on Tommy McKay's farm, continuing to follow the lie of the land and using gully thermals, they are bound to run afoul of the magpie rookery. Often the last we see of them on their regular downhill sweep is their climb for height, seeking to evade three or more swooping irate magpies, who shriek their displeasure at the harrier's presence in their patch. Yet the harrier, known to Maori as kahu, undaunted by the commotion its presence causes, returns on daily patrols, often more than once if food is short. Seated by the window, we can watch seemingly effortless flight drift them past us, a short distance above the ground, relentless eyes seeking prey or something to scavenge.

That very propensity to scavenge is not only the greatest survival skill kahu the hawk possesses, but also the biggest threat to their existence from day to day. Road kill of other species is constant where we live; pukeko, magpies, hares, rabbits, and anything from frogs and mice to starlings or goldfinches can be laid waste by cars travelling the country roads at speeds over one hundred kilometres an hour. Harrier

169

hawks will feed from the resulting carcasses with reckless urgency, often enough leaving the scene too late to avoid the car's impact. Their flight takes time to gather momentum on launching, the wide wingspan needing precious seconds to gather impetus. So their bodies lie beside the very bones and meat they were looking to feast from.

Kahu is among the most impressive of the creatures where we live. The power in flight, the ease with which they soar within a thermal updraft, the strength of their talons and hooked tearing beak, all arouse my admiration. They have been refined by evolution and perfected as predators. The muted feather colouring blends with dried or variegated foliage when the bird is on the ground, and in the air the wings, spread wide, look dark and filled with purpose. Just their shadow flickering across the water of the dam can send a clutch of ducklings fluttering for cover among the rushes and wild grasses growing at the water's edge.

Long before my family arrived here from Scotland, Ireland and England, the ancestors of this hawk I watch would have soared across bush and swamp around this area. However our 'native' harrier hawk is also an immigrant, Australian in fact, and is known there as the 'swamp harrier'. According to naturalist Tim Low, when Maori burned swamps, they created a habitat to which harriers could adapt. The birds' adaptation was accomplished to the point that they are now the predominant bird of prey in our skies, soaring over farmland that is an ideal environment for them to thrive in. They are not the only birds or wildlife to emigrate on the westerlies that blow across the Tasman Sea, but they are among the most successful.

Before the harrier cruised over the farmland developed by Pakeha settlers, Maori lived here. When my neighbour Toi Walker told me that his people named the area Waitoheariki—the place of many underground streams—I picked up how there is music in that naming. Certainly more than there is in Gladstone, the English name gazetted in the late 1800s in honour of the 'grand old man' of British (and therefore Empire) politics, who at the time was gazing out from Britannia, his island kingdom. We remain Gladstone on the maps, however, occupying a shelf of terrace country at the foot of the Maungaraki hills, looking west toward the Ruamahanga valley and the Tararua range beyond. As I write this, the Tararua ridgelines, which can be reached by a twenty-minute car ride and a three-hour walk, are covered in snow.

It's June, and these can be hungry days for kahu. In a few short weeks the paddocks either side of the Ruamahanga will supply plenty of food, in dead lambs and afterbirth, but for now, winter shadows are spread long and dark over the paddocks. Before the paddocks and the environment in which kahu could thrive, and before Maori as well, there was the forest and its birdlife. Aotearoa/New Zealand is a group

of islands that, apart from a native species of bat, grew flora and fauna devoid of mammals. Under great forest canopies, the place developed a unique character.

The soil that I dig for the garden, much modified by compost and mulch, possesses an ancient history. The rhythm of the shovel and physical effort involved in the digging brings on a good sweat, with my work already anticipating potatoes, beans, broccoli and other crops. At the same time, the repetition of the task leaves my mind free to ponder, and I can spare a thought for the past that gives my garden a geological structure to rest upon.

Far beneath our patch of dirt monumental forces meet, where the Pacific and Australian tectonic plates move against each other, causing pressures that compress and lift the sea floor to our east. The Admiral Hill road crests only five kilometres from where we live, and fossils of seashells are to be found there. They can be picked up from the roadside five hundred feet above sea level. Once they were on the floor of the Pacific Ocean.

While it doesn't cause too many problems day to day, over time, the Maungaraki hills to our east continue to crumple into the rugged limestone shapes that give them their distinctive character. Sudden ruptures of the plate interface are expressed on the earth's crust as earthquakes, and then violent movement within the landscape occurs, as it must have many, many times to form the hills we look out upon. Millions of years of such activity have formed the patch of dirt my gumboots now walk over.

Geology also tells us that our place of inland loam terraces continues to be formed by material from the South Island's Kaikoura mountain ranges. Eroded conglomerate washes out to the Pacific to be carried north by ocean currents to consolidate in reefs and sea-floor ridges off the Wairarapa coastline. It is that conglomeration of silt and limestone that successive earthquakes and tectonic plate pressure have pushed upwards and to the west to make the rugged country behind our place, and out to the east to form the wild coastline. Inside the limestone hills are aquifers supplying springs that flow from the hillsides all along the valley.

Our place has always been on the move, through the breakup of continental masses, the rise and fall of island landforms following volcanic activity, and the evolution of life as we know it.

Stories read from fossils or books tell not only of the generations of men and women who have come and gone, but also of extinct creatures that once lived on these islands. Change is the only constant, just as rain washes against rock so that it wears away. Not only human societies but also the animals that travel with colonists are likely to take advantage of change, just as kahu has.

Living as we do on 'shaky islands', at any moment an earthquake may strike, and all our monuments, or dreams of nationhood, might be rendered irrelevant. In 1855, and again in 1942, earthquakes wrecked buildings and changed landscapes in the Wairarapa. The same thing will happen again, and we are frequently warned of the possibility by the media. The hills will continue to crumple, the ocean floor to rise up forming new hills, and soil will be washed onto our terraces from those hills, for others to dig after I have gone.

Nowhere in New Zealand is immune to earthquakes. My mother used to talk about how terrifying the Murchison earthquake was in 1929. It was 7.8 on the Richter scale, and created havoc where her parents lived at Birchfield, north of Westport. She used to say that cows got caught in cracks in the earth, and we took her fears lightly. That is, until the 7.1 magnitude Inangahua earthquake struck just before daylight on 24 May 1968.

I had just left the cow shed after turning lights on and making everything ready for milking on the farm just out

173

Three of my uncles play in cracks made by the earthquake on the Kirkwood family farm at Birchfield, 1929.

of Greymouth, when, in the darkness, I heard the cows stampeding about the paddock. Then the quake struck. Down the valley, there was a spectacular show of road lights blowing. I lay down beside my dog on the heaving earth, while the cowshed power pole swayed through a big arc as I watched. Everything was moving and noisy. When the shaking subsided I looked in the cowshed, and it was a mess of stuff over the floor. I could hear rocks tumbling off the bluff kilometres away. A car raced past on the road heading to Runanga—the driver, fair flying to see if his elderly mother was okay, hit a bridge that was lifted above road level by the quake and crashed, killing himself. I went to the boss's house and he told me to go home. I did, finding my pregnant wife and my teenage cousin, who boarded with us, huddled on the lawn in blankets, afraid to go back inside the house. It was still dark. And no birds sang as the sky lightened.

I wonder what impact earthquakes have on the hawk while he soars. In all probability he cares more about his next feed—he flies above the earth at ease, designed for a dimension we only visit with the chance always that we will fall out of the sky. In all my years of looking at birds in flight, I've never seen one fall from the sky. A shotgun makes things different though, and I've seen ducks, pheasants or quail tumble earthwards when pellets from a shotgun cartridge belt into their bodies. Hawks are protected as native birdlife and normally safe from shooting, unless farmers take the law into their own hands. However, shooting is only one hazard resulting from a farmer's prejudice.

One afternoon, walking over the hills, we passed a hay barn and I was distracted by movement near a gateway. Going over, we saw that a gin trap had been set to sit on a post where magpies might alight to eat meat placed beside the trap's sprung steel jaws. Now the trap dangled, swinging on the chain anchoring it to the top of the post. With its legs caught in the steel of the trap, a hawk hung upside down, unable to do anything but beat its wings feebly as we approached. Even exhausted and weak as this bird was, the beak of a hawk is fearsome and capable of tearing the flesh off clumsy hands. Without attempting to handle it, I released the trap and let the bird fall the short distance into grass at the foot of the post. We stood back to let the bird sort itself out, and sure enough, it soon sat up lifting its proud head to gaze around. Minutes later the wings unfolded and it launched itself, a little clumsily, and flew into the hills. We continued on our walk, leaving the trap unset and dangling.

Kahu soars on thermals above the Wairarapa plain each summer, while the sun beats down forcing humans like me to seek the shade of a back porch with a cool drink in hand. A mile away to the nor'east, where the steep sides of Patrick's Bluff rise above our place, he is joined in his soaring. Taking advantage of the thermal winds near the bluff, hang gliders often launch their fragile-looking craft during summer. They circle and drift, rise toward the sun, catching light through the fabric they depend on to fly. As many as six or eight of the gliders will be in the air, when the weather is right, and they are splendid to watch. I have no desire at all to float through the air, I'll remain landlocked and looking up. The skies high over Waitoheariki are the realm of creatures designed to be up there. And sure enough, day after day he is there, riding the thermals, kahu the hawk.

Kahu is not the only predatory bird using Waitoheariki as a hunting ground. While we lived in the studio before getting our plywood and batten-clad house built, occasionally there was time for sitting on the deck in the twilight and early dark, where we'd quietly chat evenings away during that makeshift year. Not far off were big heaps of firewood and branches of trees we had felled to make a place for the buildings. On one such evening, as we just sat, letting the last light do the talking, there was a breath of flight. Silent wings flitted through the half-dark close by us. The bird sat momentarily on the wood stack, just metres away, then flew off. Moments later the mournful cry of the ruru, that little owl, was heard close by.

The silent wings, the merest shadow over the heap of black wattle limbs and leaves . . . seen, then gone, seemed mystical as much as chance. Maori have a vast array of whakatauki or proverbs to explain such random appearances, some of which feature ruru, or sometimes kahu the harrier. One of the whakatauki begins, 'tangi a te ruru ra kei te hokihoki mai e'—'the morepork's cry keeps coming to me'.

The sudden entrance followed by the silent exit of ruru that evening keeps returning to my mind when the moths are in flight and darkness is warm round us. If we are open to the possibility, I think there are moments when the elements of existence converge—when different creatures may acknowledge one another's lives—before returning to their own realm of existence. Elemental existence can take place with no before or after, just this moment—the mystic and his search for meaning may find nothing greater than a fleeting glance at the spectrum of something other, the merest glimpse. Just then on that evening, the spot we chose for building seemed the right place to be, as if the owl had cruised in to let us know 'the place' was okay with our activity. For years we have heard ruru or morepork, their eerie calls in the night always some distance from our place, more likely to be in the remnant stands of native bush up on the slopes of the Maungaraki hills.

While the advent of swamp drainage followed by pasture development has been advantageous to kahu the harrier, it has proven of little comfort to ruru, the owl, inhabitant of fringe bush lands. As a child in Ross, I saw the train arrive one day with a dead ruru across the front of the engine where it had died after a collision. That train travelled through miles of cut over native bush. I've also sighted them on stumps once or twice while out shooting opossums on the edge of the West Coast bush at night, both at Ross and up the Waiuta Valley.

Catherine and I saw one roosting in beech forest in Nelson Lakes while tramping a few years ago. They are elusive and shy of humans though, so will only seldom be caught unawares. In the last couple of years, we have not been aware of any subsequent visit, although we hear them calling up the hill, among the remnant native bush still growing on Blackwood's farm.

There are other creatures of the night in this place. Insects—moths such as the porina, a destructive pasture pest—can hatch in huge numbers, and provide food for the nocturnal little ruru. The gum emperor moth is another arrival from Australia that has spread throughout a large part of New Zealand since the first recorded landfall in 1939. The moth is the adult form of the large (up to 90 mm in length) caterpillars that can strip leaf and buds from healthy eucalypts until the tree struggles to survive, as we have noticed on several winter flowering gums we have planted here. The moths are truly beautiful, related to silk moths with distinctive eye patterns on their wings, and reaching in the female up to 130 mm wing span. At certain times of the year, or in certain weather conditions, we hear the regular thud of moths colliding with our windows after dark. They sound like soft pebbles flung against the glass. There are many varieties of moths and insects that inhabit the darkness of Waitoheariki.

And there are the creatures that feed on them. All manner of birds rely on the hatch, such as the resident fantails, and swallows, while frogs also take their share of insects down at the dam. During 2008, both Catherine's parents died— her father in June not long after going into a home, and in September her mother slipped away one morning, soon after she also had moved into a home for the elderly. A note from my journal, written between three and four a.m. one morning during the late springtime of 2008 doesn't make much sense of anything that was going on at the time.

Big enough to get lost on.

Being lost. Clambering down into the valley, not sure if it runs east, west, or anywhere. Waking, without knowing why that tree out the window has no leaves, and forgetting it is mid-winter. The cloud of knowing and not knowing, reading the titles of books on library shelves without expectation of recognition. Where am I? So many dreams when I was young, and now those dreams they wake me, night after night. The frogs are in full voice. Darkness, and filling the place where the open window lets in the world is their croaking. Randy frogs soar into expansive mode, choirs of hundreds of them, filling the tabernacle under the stars to bursting point. Their time is limited of course, without a couple of decades to try getting it right, they're getting straight down to the procreation business.

And I was lying awake. Beside me Catherine is oblivious to this orgy of sound. Sleep, a blessing if you could get it. But, seeing the Gods wanted me conscious, I threw on some clothes, and made a hot drink. With a light on, moths created a fire fight of flight and flutter the other side of the glass. All life seemed to be happening in this nocturnal planet. I thought again of that evening, not long after we arrived, she and I sitting on boxes by the building in the dark. There was wine to drink before the bugs landed in it, and we'd talked ourselves out. Silently, the owl floated past and landed on a heap of branches across the open ground.

There was so much going on. Tonight though, I thought it will be okay to read or write, eventually lethargy would creep over my brain. Bloody frogs—they're a lullaby of sorts.

There is no way back from the aging of parents. And there is no way back from our own aging, which we only understand for sure when our parents have gone. When we bought this land and settled, we were unable to return the land to what it was and the way forward seemed problematic. Our neighbours, McKays and Booths, both use chemicals and machines to maximise each hour expended on farm production. The ecology of the district is markedly altered when chemicals are introduced as a major component of customary land use. Flora and fauna become vulnerable. Some species will prove adaptable, while others fail in the attempt. It does not have to be machines or chemicals though. A pet cat can do plenty of damage, so we tend to create mischief for life around us, no matter how benign our intentions. As I wrote this paragraph, kahu floated past the window of my study, appearing without warning, and teasing my desire to photograph his wide spread wings that give a hint of his grace and power in the wind.

No matter how much we may wish to do so, there are

things in life, like a photograph of that hawk, which can't be captured. Targets can be set, aims listed, business plans created, but they are little more than the dreams of the earthbound mortals that we remain. Natural forces remain beyond our control, and have a habit of limiting our occupation of the planet. I have no problem with that. Watching the restless penetrating eye of kahu, yet again gliding past our home, I am filled with the notion that all creatures live within their limits. Sometimes, it would do no harm if humans were to accept what the limits are, rather than to chafe at the chance to be something we are not quite capable of. Tomorrow kahu may be one more road kill, but today he rides air currents capable of teasing out of me all manner of imagining. What is he really doing? Looking for a feed—same as yesterday, and the day before that. Same as he does, whether or not I watch him. Or, as Andrew suggested yesterday, with a big grin on his face, kahu is aware of my interest and just showing up to tease me. Whakarere e kahu.

Balancing acts

In the summer of 1995, I delivered a lecture at the Otago University Summer Writing School. Titled *The Isolated Writer,* it leaned heavily on the thoughts and writings of American poet Gary Snyder, while meditating on the effort it took to continue work as a poet while seldom meeting with other writers. I believed in 1995, and still do, that a great deal can be gained from working collaboratively with others. Collaboration provides mutual support, and may be nothing more than that. At other times, work where a number of people have contributed ends up with enhanced results. Yet there is still truth in the old saying that writing is a solitary craft.

At a preview of recent work by the artist Robin White, Catherine and I met others with whom she had worked to produce confrontational yet aesthetically beautiful work concerning violence to children in the Wairarapa. The wear and tear of working through intense issues on one's own can have a negative effect on the quality of creative work, so sometimes seeking out others to share the load can provide positive outcomes. For writers it always tends to be a matter of balance, however, as Snyder points out. Have too much time with other people, and the time required for writing diminishes—as he says, 'Poetry [which I take to stand for the creative arts generally] is not a social life. Nor is it a career. It's a vocation.'

Poets, like other writers, artists or composers in a small country like New Zealand, are caught between the need to create work, or do something to earn a living. Especially when the embryonic artist is starting out, income seldom flows from the pen or brush. The balancing act in preserving an artist's way of life becomes a constant ebb and flow, first in and then out of kilter. It is a matter of getting some income, and then finding time for creative production—and often enough not quite enough of either is found. The ways of achieving that middle path are various.

In 1973 Gary Snyder was asked, 'Are you a seasonal poet? Do you write more in the spring than the fall?' He replied:

Well the way I live right now, I guess I probably write more in the winter. Because in the spring I go out in the desert for a while, and I give a few readings, and then when I get back it's time to turn the ground over and start spring planting, and then right after that's done it's time to do the building that has to be done, and then when that's done it's time to start cutting firewood, and then when the firewood's done, it's just about time to start picking apples and drying them, and that takes a couple of weeks to get as many apples as possible and dry them, and then at the end of the apple season I start to harvest the garden, and a lot of canning and drying is done maybe, and then when that season passes, to chestnuts and picking wild grapes, and then I've got to put the firewood in, hunting season starts—and that winds up in about the end of October, with Halloween festivities, and then I go East for a month to read. So, December, January, and February is my time of total isolation, writing; and I don't see anybody in those months ... my family is with me, and there are neighbours to walk to.

What he was describing is a way of life, a way of being, in his place. Snyder would understand what the German philosopher Martin Heidegger is getting at when, in *Building Dwelling Thinking,* he writes that dwelling is an activity rather than an object—dwelling is what we do, more than what we buy, a verb not a noun. We buy a house, and then go about dwelling in it.

In 1928 Heidegger had a hut built on the outskirts of an alpine village called Todtnauberg in the Black Forest, a place of scenic beauty, close enough to the mountains to have an alpine climate. This site became a place for him to consider and comment on matters of rural living, or provincial themes as he called them. I suspect he aspired to live a traditional rural life there, in that active sense of dwelling. The reality was that he lived a philosopher's life, assisted by locals who were genuinely traditional villagers, whose families had roots in a place where he came to stay each summer. Most of the year he lived in the city, to fulfil his academic commitments. He had neither the time nor need to harvest produce, cut his own firewood and kill his own meat.

Yet it was in Todtnauberg that he thought his way to a position that is described by Andrew Benjamin: 'the hut for Heidegger provided the possibility for a specific type of philosophical work. Philosophy and place . . . oriented each other. As such it can be concluded that there is an important link between geography (place) and modes of thinking.' While his own life did not demonstrate the fact, Heidegger suggested in his writings that where we live determines the day-to-day balance we need to be dwelling there.

For Snyder to live where he does, and to write as he does, a trade-off that works for that place has to be adopted. Unlike Heidegger, Snyder has carried out a lot of the work himself. He does the work, along with his family, rather than paying someone else to do it. Being raised on a farm and working in practical occupations as a young man developed skills for him to build a home and live self-sufficiently in a remote area. If he lived in San Francisco, on the other hand, his concerns and the process he describes would be very different.

When Catherine and I arrived in the Wairarapa from Auckland late in 1992, each of us had to find a way of working that would suit this place. Obviously it was going to be very different from the way we had been living while working in the city. Any philosophy we may have formed over the years before our arrival was due to be shaken up in terms of specifics. We would come to describe being in Gladstone as a journey, or a never-ending process of adjustment, as we looked for some sort of balance. I had already spent years farming, gardening and learning how to live to some extent self-sufficiently. Settling into a new place should have been straight-forward, but local knowledge is invariably hard-won.

It had been ten years since I last worked at the multitude of tasks we thought needed to be done. My mind wanted to get on with things at a pace my body could no longer maintain. In the mornings I would write lists of things to be done on any particular day—mend chook house, take sheep to be shorn, buy new shovel handle, check out garage sale for sheet of particle board, borrow fencing pliers from Gil, plant carrots, build gate for front paddock, buy shelter trees, sharpen mower—and always fall short of my intentions. There was always another list—do some painting, see about framing, send away poems to *Landfall, Takahe, Bravado*—that contained tasks easily overlooked. Making poems, painting pictures, these were hobbies where we now lived. Real work was outside, making fences, building houses or using a chainsaw. For my neighbours it was just as mystifying for me to be inside reading a book while the sun was shining, as it was for me to be hanging out the washing, even if Catherine was away teaching for the day. There were other adjustments to be made.

184

Most of my experience of growing animals and plants had been in Northland and Westland, areas with plenty of rain. We now lived in a drought-prone region. Nothing grew quickly enough after planting. When the ground dried out, it was bone-jarringly hard to dig in. Things cost more than we budgeted. We had to work off the place, to create immediate cash income more than we had planned. And without rainy days, I had to train myself to stay inside to do clerical stuff like paying bills even when the sun was shining. Any sense of how to work in this place seemed to be beyond our reach at first. On a bad day everything seemed to need doing before everything else. In other words confusion ruled, and our plans, which were tentative in any case, had to be constantly adjusted. Often we talked over problems while tired at the end of the day, wondering if we had bitten off more than we could cope with.

We floundered about. Our animals died. Murray sold his farm, so we inherited Jumper his Jersey cow, a four-legged milk factory. She was placid and easy-care, had a calf, and then succumbed to liver failure. Hoppy was the next cow, Hereford-cross with a wonky hip, but easily capable of getting round as she had done for years. She also died. Even the hens failed to hatch the eggs they sat on—not once but every time. Four old ewes had lambs, or tried to. One lamb that survived birth hung itself in the forked branches of a hawthorn tree. We raised some heifers, and they had trouble calving, or even getting in calf. The entire venture of breeding looked to be mired in a mess of dead things. I'd never had a run like it. Catherine, who for various reasons had no children of her own even though she desperately wanted to, found the losses very difficult to live with in profound parts of her being.

I was telling my neighbour about the run of deaths one day. At the same time I offered a ewe to him after she was seriously damaged during my efforts to help her have a breech-birth lamb.

'Maybe you should get Auntie Sally to bless the place,' he suggested quietly.

And that is what we did. Reverend Hariata Tahana, who lived a couple of driveways down the road at that time, came and carried out a simple ritual, a blessing of our land and buildings. We started again, with live births, animals that lived, and after two or three years of struggling we began to settle a little.

Fifteen years earlier, while working in Dunedin Public Library, I'd read the philosophy of a Japanese farmer and thinker Masanobu Fukuoka. *The One Straw Revolution*, published in 1978, grew from observing the back-breaking work being done by Japanese peasant rice farmers—and his realisation that much of their work did not grow more crops. He started thinking about how plants like rice, other cereals and his mandarin trees grew, and what they needed to remain healthy. Then he modelled his farming practice on the needs of the plants and soil, rather than what 'needed to be done', with the result that there were fewer jobs needing to be done. His book had been a revelation to me when I read it, and now at Gladstone it was time I reconsidered the wisdom in his words. What were the jobs that really needed to be done? What jobs kept the chooks healthy, made the garden grow best or produced milk from the cow? There are times to sweat, and times to think. If we wanted to stay on this land we had to put in the necessary thought, to work with the land not against it. Rather than breaking in land to make it perform as we would wish, a more sustainable option is to go with what it offers.

Fukuoka's thinking had side benefits in addition to ample production. I tried to shift his belief to this place, where not cutting grass provided habitat for lizards and frogs, and mulch allowed good bugs to grow alongside bad bugs, while birds arrived to feed on both, in the untidy areas. Rotting mulch provided a place for much more than just the growth of trees to take place. More life meant a healthier place, while the slightest increase of diversity provided additional positive outcomes. In the long run, we were developing and operating in a cyclical process that appears sustainable. With the desire for tidiness and control taken out of the equation, suddenly there were fewer tasks to be carried out. What the neighbours might think was another concern altogether, out with their spray units and machinery each weekend maintaining the look of the district. Laziness has no place in this rural area, and tidiness equals the absence of laziness. Everybody understands production, though.

A number of studies of traditional farming systems have established that mechanisation and increased production come with the price of reduced leisure for the farmer. There is a passage in *The One Straw Revolution* in which Fukuoka laments the loss of time for contemplation:

> There is no time in modern agriculture for a farmer to write a poem or compose a song. The other day I was surprised to notice, while I was cleaning the little village shrine, that there were some plaques hanging off the wall. Brushing off the dust and looking at the dim and faded letters, I could make out dozens of *haiku* poems. Even in a little village such as this, twenty or thirty people had composed *haiku* and presented them as offerings. That is how much space people had in their lives in the old days. Some of the verses must have been several centuries old. Since it was that long ago they were probably poor farmers, but they still had leisure to write *haiku*. Now there is no one in this village with enough time to write poetry.

On this place of ours, there had to be time for at least one farmer to write poetry. That was my identity, I was a poet. Time passed, and we did develop a pattern of sorts, sporadic breathing spaces in which we could consider our position. We learned a few things along the way, and continue to do so. Ever so gradually we moved into a different space, one that seemed more like co-existence with this piece of land on which we built a house, planted trees and reared animals. On a bad day we still had to live with the knowledge that the sense of place described by Wallace Stegner (with reference to an essay by Wendell Berry) is beyond our reach:

> He is not talking about the kind of location that can be determined by looking at a map or a street sign ... He is talking about the knowledge of place that comes from working in it in all weathers, making a living from it, suffering from its catastrophes ... [from all] that you, your parents and grandparents, your all-but-unknown ancestors have put into it.

And I have to wonder if perhaps Berry is asking too much of our contemporary situation? The continuity he proposes has been lost. Our contemporary postcolonial culture is so disrupted, on the move, almost incoherent with change and very new in terms of generations of settlement. We are also in a situation governed more often by commodity prices than values such as ecological balance or sustainability as far as I can see. No wonder there were days when I'd be left standing in a dishevelled state, having sworn myself luridly to a standstill, absolutely beside myself with frustration and a sense of being a cosmic clown, unable to slow down yet knowing I was rushing and making mistakes because of it.

Broken tools, paintings that didn't work or poems that went nowhere fast eventually forced me to take stock. Was I just going about things the hard way, trying to live in some sort of harmony with the land while developing creative practices in the arts? It is a denial of common sense to keep pushing for results. The land takes its own time, cows move at their own pace and plants will grow according to the season. They are perfectly happy without my input and desire to hasten the process.

Living in this place may require an understanding of what it is to dwell in the way Heidegger uses the term, and might benefit from a different approach to working the land as Fukuoka suggests—but is that enough? Dwelling within a traditional vernacular requires an attitude of mind as much as skills. It is not just what we know, but also how we go about it, Michel de Certeau says in *The Practice of Everyday Life*. He believes a 'third knowledge' exists in an uneasy relationship with the disciplines of science and philosophy. My understanding is that that sort of practical, 'third' knowledge is invariably local, or centred on place. De Certeau calls it 'know-how', a type of making do that we traditionally admire in rural New Zealand. We would call the attribute common sense, or having a number-eight-wire philosophy. He goes into detail, suggesting that an historical role of the artisan/craftsman was to use their know-how to create society's materially mundane requirements, but that over time technology has been developed to such an extent that everyday use for crafts is no longer widespread. Why use a painstakingly acquired craft when it is possible to get into a car, drive to The Warehouse, and buy an object such as a coffee mug made overseas, for less than it costs to obtain raw materials and make it yourself? What is more, there is always time to be saved. It seems we no longer need to live locally, and traditional or place-based ways of life are endangered.

Where craft does persist, it is still to do with having a knack, possessing know-how that is unspoken and seemingly undefined. It is the type of knowledge that we suppose is picked up by association with other practitioners, and is synonymous with traditional craft, folklore or myth. Knowledge is owned by insiders, and is notable for being local, possessed by those with a sense of place. The knack for a type of work can be described as using an art—the art of tight fencing, building plumb walls, cooking roast lamb, spinning merino fleece. The art comes from doing the job with 'know-how', so that it is better than just adequate, possessing, as it will, a personal touch.

We built our first house in Gladstone fifteen years ago, in our spare time. Recycled timber was used as often as possible, and I designed the interior with Catherine as we went, after the shell was erected. While I have no formal training as a carpenter, landscaper or architect, I've picked up stuff along the way. My attributes may only be patience, and a willingness to work hard using my 'know-how'. Working as a builder just comes naturally, each finished task, while far from perfect, is given approval with the frequently heard self-effacing site talk. 'A blind man'd be pleased to see it' or 'Yuh can't build a silk purse out of a sow's ear.'

Other local individuals have acquired the knack of lighting gorse fires, digging post holes without strain, shearing clean and fast, making fine bread rolls, knitting a jersey without a pattern, or keeping ancient machinery going. In some cases they possess 'green fingers'. If one has the knack, one has likely acquired it without much formal instruction, often from parents with similar skills. The learning of vernacular tasks is characterised by continuity that accepts, rather than challenges, traditional processes. Being local, in the dwelling sense, is not an intellectual exercise one can impose by willpower or reason. An individual simply grows into a state of being local. All of this takes time, and acceptance that the process cannot be hurried.

Stories are paramount in defining place. To be a local is to be part of the group that knows the stories of a place. The narrative of the vernacular carries with it assumptions of insider knowledge. In other words, stories provide what de Certeau calls the 'decorative container' for everyday practices. Stories provide boundaries within which to operate, as well as the genealogy of a place. There is an art to telling these stories, and some people carry the gift with more flair than others. When my father died, among stories told about him were those detailing what a good storyteller he had been, but he wasn't local.

Gladstone has men and women who tell the stories, each with their own style and flair. De Certeau suggests that their storytelling acts 'as an index of particulars—the poetic or tragic murmurings of the everyday' of this place. The stories sustain the vernacular, a local way of being. Their yarns or anecdotes have a style, most often understated, that give a glimpse of local practice. Without them the vernacular could well have no expression or continuity. Yarning, or chatting together, is also a way in which change can be verbalised and absorbed. In that sense, storytelling keeps the locals 'up with the play'.

When a 'local' tells me a yarn about the store, with its shelves of screw-top jars, dust and dim recesses holding one of virtually everything anyone could dream of asking for—and how Arnold would say 'hang on a minute' and disappear into the shadows to reappear before long holding a requested item as if it were an ancient trophy—then I am aware that after eighteen years here, I have really only just arrived. The yarn is of a time ten or twenty years before my arrival, by someone who knew Gladstone as a place with a community store, petrol pumps, few newcomers and, not long before that, shingle roads. Just recently another friend told a story about a couple who had been in the district for six months, and they hadn't met them yet. The sense of loss is palpable, for a time when everyone knew each other in this place.

I suppose that is why being part of a place is important, because only then do I get to hear the stories. If I keep shifting all the time, a way of living full of short-term solutions develops. As the philosopher of place Edward Casey has put it, 'To live is to live locally, and [to] know is first of all to know the place one is in.'

Building our house at Red Roofs took years, and we moved into it with work still to be finished, which is not an unusual story. We planted trees, erected fences, and farmed the acreage with cattle, sheep and poultry. I started learning what it meant to stay in one place for more than a year or two, after a lifetime of moving on. I had to give up fixing things by abandoning them to make another fresh start. I also had to stop rushing in with stopgap solutions to problems. Discussing options with others and gradually deciding on the best course of action was a habit to be cultivated. There were still plenty of new things to be done, however, because staying put did not mean becoming stagnant.

We celebrated the arrival of the new millennium at a hut high in the Cupola Basin, looking out over the mountain tops of Nelson Lakes National Park. Within days we returned home. Later that summer, we sat and talked with friends in the long grass of our front paddock. What a good house site the paddock now was, how fine a dam would look in the swampy area down the gentle slope in front of us, how the chestnut trees we'd planted along the gully were growing. We sipped on chardonnay they had brought over to share. Again we looked out across space to mountain tops, the Tararua range. This was turning into our place, but what came next?

It was the Tararuas painted in reference to Gallipoli and my developing sense of a personal history here that I was working on when I developed intolerance to oil paints, turpentine, and any chlorine or petroleum-based fumes during 2004, and there was no real improvement for a large part of 2005. It got to the point where walking through the household cleaners or soaps aisle at a supermarket could make me fight for breath. We recognised the need to do something if we wanted to remain in Gladstone. Our alternative lifestyle would be unable to be maintained indefinitely if one of us was sick most of the time. It was time to act.

By the end of 2005 we had sold seven of our ten acres, along with the red-roofed house we had sweated and laboured to build. The following year we studied, while carpenters built a new home on the same spot where we had shared wine with friends that earlier summer. Our three-acre front paddock of the previous ten years was to become our dwelling place— on the south side we could walk through a recently planted olive grove to the house and, from windows facing north we'd see the chestnut trees, backed by a woodlot of timber trees planted by us over fifteen years ago. The new dam so often seen in my vision of this place would be filled with winter rainwater, runoff from paddocks where sheep browse and hens fossick. We moved into the house during a summer that marked the start of eighteen months of drought.

It seems natural, when leaving behind part of our land, and all but the story of building our own home, that I would want to think about a 'sense of place'. There has recently been a reconsidering of what we're up to—linked in part to death of our parents, my gradual discovery of unstoried ancestors, but also a sense of settling and acceptance of where we are. The link between staying in one place and a growing sense of self is no accident. I respond to artist Roni Horn's desire for 'a plain knowledge of oneself, a kind of common sense gathered through repeated exposures to distilling experiences . . . peace of mind in the world as it is and not as I imagine it.' After the ill health in 2004, it seemed important to live more within my physical means, attending more to that 'plain knowledge' of self and acceptance of my own inner resources. At last I am beginning to like the simplicity in the idea of a pragmatic and sustainable relationship with a particular place.

The dam, sheep tracks, the woodlot, fencelines, gardens and buildings become the locale of storytelling. Wild creatures

193

come and go, frogs croak on the dam, hares run the gauntlet of mown grass and lizards hang out under old totara posts overgrown by grass. There is birdlife: the shining cuckoo arrives in spring, ducks occupy the dam from late winter, tui arrive to feed off winter flowering gum, take off then return for flowering flax. Cabbage trees blossom abundantly or with restraint depending on the fluctuation of rainfall. Patterns emerge that add to the rhythm of living here.

It is four decades since I had to leave behind the dream of being a full-time farmer while recovering from a severe bout of leptospirosis. That young man's lesson of loss I've had to learn over and over. Nonetheless my life in this particular place is slowly encompassing a 'nuanced local knowledge' just as the highly popular author, Michael Pollan, suggests a successful farmer maintaining a sustainable practice must. On a good day it can be sufficient to look at the trees we've planted; for firewood, nuts, fruit, olives—and be thankful. Not only farmers have to live knowing where they live—we all do.

Part of knowing where we live in this rural enclave is found if I try to answer the same question as that put to Gary Snyder in 1973, 'When do you write?'

Or perhaps the question if addressed to Catherine would be, 'Do you have sufficient time to attend to the making of music or art?'

I find we both attempt to tune into a seasonal rhythm. Many of the tasks with which we fill our days are decided by hours of sunlight, the presence of wind, the absence of water or something else that is climatic, local or otherwise beyond our control.

Imagine that now it is springtime, and the ewes lamb— or this year for us, our one ewe has her lamb. The sheep (we have a couple of wethers) are shorn, and the garden dug over. We have to spend time cutting grass, which we won't have to do once summer heat burns off leaf. Grass becomes a fire hazard if left to grow rank after going to seed so we are obliged to keep it under some sort of control. Southerly storms come through and that means late frosts, so we have to plant seedlings in accordance with weather which varies a little every year. Before the ground dries out and becomes hard is the time to do any digging of post holes or drains. If we have any calves, then they have to be fed their bucket of milk every morning and evening during spring. The more sheep or calves we raise, the less grass we have to cut, but the more tending to animals we have to carry out—just another balancing act. Springtime is a chance to welcome warmth in the sun, more hours of daylight and more work.

With summer we have to cut firewood and make sure that seedling trees do not become overgrown with grass and weeds. Hot dry nor'west winds can desiccate foliage and shrivel vegetables in the garden. Watering plants becomes an evening preoccupation for weeks on end. Clucky hens need to be secluded in a separate hutch sitting on their dozen eggs, in order to hatch a clutch of chickens, ensuring a supply of cockerels for meat and pullets to take over as laying hens next winter. As fruit comes available there is a chance to preserve or freeze apples, raspberries, apricots and plums in packs for times of short supply later on. Because the orchard we planted was sold with the red-roofed house, we will plant more fruit trees next winter.

The wool from shearing is taken to be carded, so it can be spun as evenings become longer through autumn, a time which sees us start using the stored firewood. Once again we are heating our water without electricity because we have a wet back on our fireplace. Pumpkins, potatoes and other summer vegetables are harvested before frosts. Winter crops, brassica like cabbage, cauliflower and broccoli are planted. The compost heaps are spread on the garden, and the chook run cleaned out and that material thrown on the compost heap to rot down for next year. About the time frosts start we harvest chestnuts and almonds. Once the walnut trees grow big enough to have more than the couple of nuts they have managed so far, there will be another harvesting chore.

In late May or early June, that time between autumn and winter, the olives are harvested. The crop is taken to Martinborough for pressing, and the oil brought home to be stored and bottled once it has settled. Any time after that the olive trees can be pruned. Pine nuts can be gathered, but we have not really developed an efficient method of dealing with them yet. We wait until the almonds have lost their leaf before their pruning. Hay is fed to the calves now as the weather starts to cool. Feijoas fall from the trees to be gathered, any time from now on.

And then it is winter. During dry weather we carry out maintenance of fences. There are trees to plant and animals to feed. This coming winter we mean to plant more shelter trees to the west of the almond orchard, and also some more fruit trees which will include plums and feijoas. The garden gets dug over, and weeds are kept away from the brassica crops. Just as we do all year, the weeds get thrown over the fence into the chook run for them to scratch amongst.

At certain times of year Catherine records sounds such as birds staking out their territory, then finding mates, and after that the noisy bustle of raising broods until the chicks fledge. If she doesn't make the effort at the right time, the birds will be busy elsewhere. I submit work when there are deadlines, and try to save the mornings for writing. Both of us are often constrained by deadlines, and they do not necessarily suit what is going on outside the back door on the land. Timetables of places to show art or publish writing are not conditioned by seasonal needs. Poetry readings and teaching opportunities occur when they happen along. When work arrives we have to decide if we should take it, and so the balancing act continues—an existential dance, which gives us busy times, and idle days only if we turn our back on tasks to be done. To an outsider it may seem we are living such an interesting life, yet on a bad day the schedule feels relentless, as if we endlessly play catch-up.

Chores are what connect us to this place, however. The daily involvement has ways of providing the observations we adopt and assemble into the story of our lives. Events occur within the accumulation of chores or harvesting of food, like finding a nest in a tree being cut for firewood and seeing the thread off an old shirt woven into the intricate web of moss and twigs. Finding the twigs of a 'dead' seedling hiding new shoots at its base produces another task, and pulling weeds and mulching round the fragile signs of life are always jobs to enjoy. This morning the kingfisher is back on the stump beside the dam—I know it's there because I heard its cry. It probably heard, as we did a couple of nights ago, frogs croaking out of the darkness down there at the water's edge. Before long that kingfisher will be wreaking havoc among the tadpoles swimming in the weeds growing around the edge of the dam.

The chores that need doing provide continuity, and involvement, on any small block of land. We manage our lives round what needs to be done next, just as plenty of our friends do, and we have had to start learning how that works best for this block of land. We are still learning.

Dreaming the wood pigeons' return

An acquaintance tried talking to me recently while I split some firewood freshly cut out of our woodlot. That old splitting axe was one of the best tools I ever spent money on. This fellow was lamenting the ease with which the heavy head of the axe went through each block of black wattle taken from the heap to stand momentarily on the chopping block. One or two judicious questions and it turns out that he'd been having a spot of bother splitting some old blocks of gum trees felled and left to dry.

'Ah huh,' I offered. 'You have to split eucalypts as soon as possible after they're felled.'

'Why?'

'Something to do with the fibres in the grain . . . as the wood dries.' I leaned over to grasp another piece of wattle, laying it end-up on the block.

'How do you get to know these things?' This wasn't a question really, but plaintive, as if some sleight of hand was being practised on him. 'Where can I find out what to do?'

I can't recall what I offered in reply.

In nature, it seems most creatures are born with a set of instincts pretty much hard-wired, conditioning their response to daily events. Experience can be added to the mix for a select few, learning from their mistakes by doing as their parents do, assuming their mistakes aren't terminal. The élite of young creatures grow to become canny older creatures. For human beings, survival seems to be a bit more complex. There are things to learn, even about the way learning takes place. We tangle the obvious in words with no trouble at all. There are so many pitfalls, and a lot to learn for survival in the urban environments where most of us live. If later on in life, with a few dollars in the bank, we arrive at a decision to 'escape' to a block of land in a rural setting, a whole lot more has to be learned. In fact there is more to know than can ever be learned. Moving into a rural way of life where we interact directly with the natural landscape, new things about our own nature are inevitably learned as well.

Splitting wood is something I've done since Dad got me using the tomahawk to cut kindling wood for fire-starting, probably not long after I was first going to school—maybe even before. I don't remember being taught how to split wood, it just grew up alongside me, like digging holes, or fishing. The 'know-how' just sort of 'arrived' in place. Not like Annie Dillard who one day realised that when the axe is swung, one doesn't strike for the top of the block to be split—no, the idea is to swing through the block, as if the split will definitely occur, hit for the chopping block underneath. One has to commit to the total act. Dillard's description of this epiphany is lyrical. But then, I think craftily, she was probably splitting straight-grained cedar or pine, not a stubborn dried-out block of peppermint gum. She spent her childhood in a city. A fair bit of mine was lived alongside a railway track on the outskirts of various New Zealand townships. We learned early to be self-sufficient in different ways, with habits that could easily be redundant in a city flat, like stacking firewood in ways to let the air through it so that it would be dry come winter.

The knack of doing things is acquired by a mix of experience, observation, talking to old people, growing up with an assortment of tasks to be done—and then more experience. This haphazard way of transferring knowledge is great for providing stability and tradition, but things can fall apart when innovation or new ideas are called for. I'm thinking now about something specific—the way we care for our land, as farmers, owners, new settlers or old. On my desk where I write this note are three books I've yet to read. The subject of one is Eliot Porter's photography, a sumptuous visual feast reminding us of wild places often close to the American towns he lived in. Many of the photo sites are now altered by development of one sort or another, the Glen Canyon dam on the Colorado River system arguably the best known example of a hydro-electric dam altering the landscape of America. We have similar examples in New Zealand, especially on the Waikato and Clutha River systems.

The second book, waiting to be reviewed, is titled *Wetlands of New Zealand: A Bittersweet Story*. The bulk of the country's swamp and wetland has now been drained, to serve as farmland or, in some cases, as sites for urban development. Down the valley from where I live, swamp land has been drained for agriculture, and a small stream has been turned to flow in a different direction through drained paddocks towards an entirely new destination some kilometres away from what used to be swamp and its original destination.

And the third title, *Rare Wildlife of New Zealand*, includes writing about examples of all types of flora and fauna—fish, birds and plants. In a sense they are all concerned with the same underlying theme, which is the story of change, and the way environmental diversities tend to be altered or depleted by human encroachment or intervention. I'll read and review the last two titles for the local weekly newspaper, and further enhance some locals' suspicions that I'm a stirrer and a hippie, if not a downright 'greenie'. I have believed for a long time that environmental issues need talking about, and I am not alone in that.

The other night at a friend's house-warming party, a chance conversation took place that has stayed with me. We were chatting, as you do with a glass of wine or can of beer in hand, idling away a hot evening. Jobs, weather, the same old stuff filled the air, until someone started talking about their tree planting programme on the family farm. So many native species they'd planted, and so many of the plantings had died. Conditions can be a bit rough, with wind, summer drought and late frosts all conspiring to make starting out hard for young life. Farm animals, birds and trees all struggle in this climate at times.

One hundred miro, karaka and other flowering natives had given up trying over the preceding summer.

'A year wasted,' she said. 'We planted them specially to attract native wood pigeons.'

The kereru, or wood pigeon, once common in this area was now seldom seen.

'All farmers are greenies at heart,' someone commented. The conversation veered off, and before long turned to water, or lack of it. Often enough these days, chat does focus on water, rain or lack of both, round here. In late January while I write this, the tankers are delivering water to houses out of town, and most days we see or rather hear the heavy vehicles rumble by. We live in dry country, not Aussie dry like it is where my son Gareth lives, south of Melbourne, but dry enough to make me long for long moist autumn days, when summer heat seems to stretch forever into winter. The Wairarapa is dry enough for farmers who milk cows or grow grapes and/or olives to spend big money on irrigation systems, with powerful pumps sucking water out of the region's rivers and aquifers.

Then the subject changed a little and I really was listening. Plans were under way to dam the headwaters of the

Ruamahanga River in the Tararua foothills, before it winds down to meander across the Wairarapa plain.

'When you think of all the water that flows downstream in floods every winter,' was one comment, 'imagine what that could do for us if it was available each summer.'

I am reminded of a remark made by a successful dairy farmer, which was repeated to me last year.

'A drop of water that reaches the sea after flowing down the Ruamahanga is water wasted as far as I'm concerned.'

Back then Andy and I were talking about how easy it seems to consider our human situation as separate from the natural world 'out there'. And fair enough, it is difficult to imagine how any action locally would have an influence globally. We just have to remind ourselves that there are now many local actions taking place all over the planet in the twenty-first century. Not everyone is like our friends at the party, planting miro, kahikatea, tawa, karaka and other trees for native birds to feast on in years to come.

Later today, Catherine and I intend to travel half an hour north of where we live at Gladstone to walk into Roaring Stag Lodge, a trampers' hut situated in a valley where the Ruamahanga flows out of the mountains. Further down that valley the river flows through gorges before meandering past Masterton and other towns toward the sea. That valley seems a likely spot for such a water scheme. Is this the site of the proposed dam? I have no idea. It is certainly a pretty good spot to walk in, and remains a habitat for wildlife seldom seen on the plains where farmland or townships occupy available space.

We confront problems such as water shortage, or at a personal level, wood splitting, with an assumption it is not about us or our personal habits. There is often no consideration of having to modify our use of resources.

'If the settlers had chainsaws, we would not see a tree standing now,' Hank my elderly neighbour often says, in his Dutch accent. He is referring to the hills over which the sun rises to shine down on our properties during summer months.

Now we want more water, because the land dries out terribly since we cleared it of trees and drained the swamps. On the other hand we also want the wood pigeons back, in trees that bear fruit for them to eat. Maybe it is possible to dam the river, and even get the wood pigeons back into the trees. But then what? Will we want something else in the region? Probably we will.

Not long ago another dam site was proposed, but an action group of concerned residents opposed the idea and the proposal of a dam bringing prosperity to all was put to one side. Apparently, though, an alternative scheme is due to be hatched, and ideas of what could be done with surplus water haven't gone away. An obvious objection to putting any major dam in the Wairarapa hills would have to be our location in an area of multiple fault lines. In 1855 an earthquake measuring 8.2 on the Richter scale created a rift over two metres high along the western foothills. A lake was formed in the northern hills of Wairarapa by that earthquake. The lake is noted these days for kowhai blossom and birdlife around its shores each spring. Tui feed on nectar in idyllic surroundings with numbers increasing each year. Scars of that earthquake still exist, but are well clothed now with natural regeneration. The scars demonstrate, however, that nature is capable of moving any man-made structure such as a dam. Systems of natural life are complex, and we meddle with them at some peril.

The present generation didn't clear the bush in this district, but our fathers or their fathers did. They would have seen numerous wood pigeons flying round in all probability. Quite likely they also had some untidy corners where swampy ground proved to be a breeding site for insect pests, and dark gullies with rubbish growing in them. There, where burning off hadn't reached, some scrub probably grew berries and bird tucker for wood pigeons. My grandfather and great grandfather were more than likely too busy digging drains and fencing new pasture to notice when the last wood pigeon flew over their land, or fed in their trees. Either that or they shot it for pigeon stew. One hundred years later, I have only once in twenty years seen a pigeon flying over our land. We have planted hundreds of trees on the four hectares we initially bought, but we were thinking of shelter and firewood more than birdlife. Now we have many native birds, tui among them, but no pigeons. We regularly plant more trees, and just as regularly cut some as firewood for a self-perpetuating cycle has developed.

Firewood is a summer job out here for most of us, and maybe it is time for my friend to talk to one or two locals about what goes on in the district as far as his requirements are concerned. There may be a forester who is pruning trees or thinning a plantation. Is there a need to timetable the cutting of firewood so that the necessary hours can be spent splitting that eucalypt when it is felled, rather than later on? Who knows, a farmer may welcome the carting away of a few trailer loads of willow that is clogging up a creek bordering his paddocks. A couple of neighbours might want to team up and get the job done in less time. Maybe he can grow firewood trees that coppice and don't need splitting? Maybe someone will suggest hiring a hydraulic wood splitter to help in harvesting the old dried-out gum. It would be a shame to waste such good-quality firewood, just because an axe can't drive through the blocks that lie in long grass waiting to be used. Solving the firewood problem, or at least the attitude to the firewood, may not seem like a major step, but all change has to start somewhere.

*

When it comes to mucking round with our environment, ordinary questions are often barbed with complexity. Simple answers might be beyond our reach, and any knowledge we have, tentative. Our best intentions may be suspect—yet we can at least try to do small chores and everyday tasks in a semblance of harmony with our surroundings. Admitting the need to adapt could be a place to start—things in the natural world change anyway, with the puff of a breeze, the breaking of a wave. Sometimes my own pressing needs may not contribute to the ecological balance of where I live. Perhaps economic advantage is best balanced against other, longer-term benefits.

Firewood, native pigeons and dam water are only three strands of the woven unfinished story of this place. This winter, close to our own small dam, I count on planting a few more trees. Given time, they may provide wild berries and fresh growth for future generations of wood pigeons and other birdlife.

wood pigeon
fantail brown teal
shearwing plover
goldfinch skylark kingfisher
doves grey warbler thrush   blackbird
waxeye sparrow magpie pukeko tui
kahu - harrier hawk
Birds I've seen here at Waitoheariki
in the air, on the water and   some are
among the trees — or feeding   visitors, some
along the grass verges   resident
grey heron mallard duck red pollen
rosella   shoveller d. barnevelde hens
little shag paradise d. shining cuckoo
chaffinch green finch welcome swallow
Canada geese black swan little grebe
morepork - ruru starling black-backed gull

There is a postscript to be read on a page taken from one of my journals, recording birds that I have seen here. A few weeks ago my neighbour told me he spotted a pair of crows in their characteristic lumpy flight, ploughing the air across his paddocks this year. Things will change again with their arrival, as they drift south from Hawkes Bay where they are now well established.

Last week, in the early evening of mid-October, we sat in a friend's kitchen looking out to where big old tree lucernes dominate the hillside. Wood pigeons flew over to land heavy and clumsily in the high branches of spring growth. We estimated close to ten birds were feeding on something up there in the high growth before settling down for the night. Those friends live only seven kilometres away from our place, so wood pigeons are not far away.

Meanwhile we will take what is on offer, our dawn chorus, and evensong at dusk, after the wind has dropped. That, and the trees busy with birds rustling round, making ready for nightfall.

The new dam:
story of an intervention

In the autumn of 2006, before the foundations had time to settle into the clay providing the base plate for our new house, the digger arrived to create the dam. We wanted to re-create something where an original dam was probably hacked out of soil with pick and shovel decades before. Through a process of passing seasons, and the splayed hooves of Aberdeen Angus cattle degrading the banks as they waded in for drinking water each summer, the dam deteriorated. Water muddied, became infested by plant growth, then eventually, a rush- and weed-filled swamp of indeterminate depth evolved.

Within six hours the digger removed sludge, forming a new dam with steep deep walls, and a sturdy face to hold the many thousands of litres of winter rain that run off the hills behind our small acreage. And 'Yogi' the driver was gone, heading off to the next job. Dam builders are sought after each autumn for their ability to create potential water storage for use during summers in this drought-prone region. Without dams, many farmers here would often be unable to raise the livestock numbers they do. On small blocks of land similar to the one where we live, there is less need for dams. They become cosmetic, an indulgence justified by the requirements of landscaping, perhaps the desire to create a water feature. They are all, regardless of their purpose, an example of human intervention.

But then, the plains of Wairarapa are a formidable example of human meddling in more ways than creating sites where water ponds. Original forest cover has been milled as timber or clear felled and burned. Swamps are drained. Irrigation and the plough have been used, are being used, in acts of economic transformation.

Yet it is possible something more basic, older than economic imperatives, moves land owners in their approach to house sites. Australian author Tim Low says, 'wherever man settles he tends to maintain forest edge communities in the vicinity of his habitations'. He continues, 'when people move into forests they make clearings, and when they reside on plains they grow trees'. In my community that tendency can be seen all round us, as closer settlement reclaims the large paddocks used for the business of farming. People buy a few paddocks, maybe an acre, maybe four hectares, perhaps a bit more. They then plant trees, or modify those that already exist. In effect, a conversion of locally productive farmland is carried out to produce a pseudo forest/savannah interface. Low does not mention that those clearings also had to be near water, the other essential element to sustain life. Many a modern development is designed for water to be seen among the trees; it is not quite sufficient for it to arrive from a tap. To create this psychological oasis, so much part of an innate human desire, there are times when excessive resources seem to be used for a relatively limited return.

As individuals we seldom spend time on the question Wendell Berry raises when he asks, 'What will this do to our community?' Real estate agents do all they can to encourage this tendency, of people to seek out the rural idyll, but the dream often turns sour once the amount of work involved surfaces. The average length of time a smallholding is owned before it is sold is said to be less than three years.

New arrivals, disillusioned by constant chores, decide to head back to town, and the agent can sell and resell the same block as the ownership recycles. The sign will go back up in town—'Be quick! Your chance to live the dream is now.' Lifestyle farmers are the real estate agents' 'cash cow', and the community, or the land it occupies, are low on the list of priorities. Land as commodity, and potential profit, overrules land as a responsibility to be cared for.

I've been thinking about the dam recently. Rather, I've been thinking about its role in our lives. After months of summer drought, we've had rain and the dried-out clay walls are beginning to sink into the water—a fascinating optical illusion that denies the rising water level. We have no apparent or practical use for a dam. So, I have to ask myself, why build one? Is it really to create an edge of forest environment? At the edge of the forest do I need water—in a creek, lagoon, billabong, wadi, estuary, spring, or even a dam? Is my subconscious at work in that way? Geoff Park claims that the meeting of water with land, in the company of groves of trees, invokes the spell of childhood memories. Are we really that vulnerable to the pull of subconscious

desires dredged up from distant childhood, or even further back?

The idea that we are attracted to surroundings that combine trees with open spaces where water lies conjures up questions about the way we not only think, but also act, as citizens of the twenty-first century. The human brain has been adapting and evolving over many millions of years, long before humans came on the scene in fact. There also appear to be three distinct phases of development: reptilian, paleomammalian and neomammalian. According to Anthony Stevens, the reptilian brain perpetuates the automatic, compulsive urgency characteristic of much human behaviour, for example, our survival instinct of fight or flight. In other words, there are times we are conditioned to act according to the directives of our earliest evolved brain cells in ways that are primitive and held in common with reptilian life forms. Some ways we respond to a situation link to information hardwired before we left the swamp.

Then, our paleomammalian region of the brain, to put it very crudely, moves us beyond the instinctual, by providing us with memory among other things. So we can remember the results of our fear and flight response. Finally, and moving through another few million years without a blink, what takes me or you beyond the mentality of frogs or birds (and beyond the reach of my sheepdog's mind) is possession of a neocortex or neomammalian brain. This area capable of cognition and perceptual processes ensures we can justify as well as remember our instinctive responses to events. Each level of the brain is dependent on processes buried in the evolutionary journey of the entire organism.

Even in contemporary society, everything we do still depends on interactions from all three parts of our presently evolved brain. Large segments of human activity, of new situations and day-to-day decision-making, are carried out using a brain that developed automatic responses before our ancestors even descended from the trees. There is the snag. We are not always reasonable. Times of stress see most people respond at such a basic or subconscious level, they describe their actions as 'out of character'.

I want to reconsider our position, to return via the new dam and the minimal sketch of our human minds to the proposal that we either go back to nature or forward to the future, to the idea that the universe is indifferent to humanity. Dickens' character Mr Jarndyce was not quite so distant or indifferent in his assumption. He was unable to resist allowing himself the comforting metaphor of the universe as *'parent'*. Not such a great step away from accepting the presence of a God, really; not necessarily benevolent or all powerful, but certainly out there somewhere in the wings, the great security blanket in the sky perhaps. Furthermore, the premise that humans have evolved to understand and intervene in the process of indifferent nature is similarly requesting that readers recognise the presence of an omnipotent overview, a supreme purpose to existence. This time humans are placed in the box seat, however, complete with the crown and sceptre of knowledge dispensed with reason.

Of course we intervene—but with understanding? I hesitate to say yes. Our assumption of the interventionist role has led to a game of consequences in which annihilation of our species could easily feature. We are successful as a species in that we proliferate, but the idea that we intervene from a platform of understanding is debatable. 'Understanding of what?' my own reason has to ask.

Our minds are too multilayered, various and complex, to assume our most recently acquired mental attribute, the power of reason, should preside unopposed over other successful, even though archaic, mental mechanisms.

Rather, we could walk in wonder, and be gentle in our guess of what we may and may not understand. When Darwin writes, 'from so simple a beginning endless forms most beautiful and most wonderful have been and are being evolved', he is suggesting we are only a part in a process of continuing change. Darwin was awake to the sense of that great drama, which life in its profligate energy and magnitude is capable of producing. He saw that there is much that lies beyond our highly reasoned yet ultimately simplistic comprehension.

I have suggested that the intervention of our putting in a dam would be considered normal practice, within the context of the ecology of a small acreage in this district. Others put down bores, using unspecified quantities of water from the aquifer flowing underground. People bulldoze house sites, erect fences, carve driveways across slopes and plant all manner of exotic species. Ostensibly, they are making a capital investment for such economic reasons as family welfare. I am not ready to ask my neighbours if any of them are living out a subconscious need to create an edge-of-woodland scenario with their manicured, shaped-to-fit, arbitrary boundaries, their striving for individuality of design in similar formats.

Our present actions are layered upon decades of previous activity. A driveway may overlay an old cattle track, a bore be dug to replace a series of non-functional dams, a house be built on an exposed site to gain a view, where an abandoned house was tucked out of the wind in a gully. David Suzuki says: 'we human beings have a remarkable desire and ability to shape our surroundings for our convenience and comfort. And because we have the inventive and technological capacity to do it, any failure to exploit a natural "resource" is deemed a waste . . . But all too often we fail to consider a project's impact beyond its immediate locale or payoff, and we end up paying heavy ecological costs.'

So what about our little pond on three acres? Rainfall and the consequent runoff will fill the dam most winters, and the overflow will carry any surplus water down the shallow gully in which it has been built. Once, native bush would have structured a very different landscape. Tree-covered slopes would have caused the gully to hold more water, as runoff would have been slower, and the gully shadier. Old growth would have fallen over the water course and formed temporary dams round which the flow would have meandered. Only with cultivation and clear felling, replacing bush with pasture, has the gully taken on the smooth-sided direct lines of flow we inherited from previous land users.

Two years ago, the few swamp weeds that showed where the old dam had been were a hazard to livestock. Sheep or cattle got bogged there trying for something juicy, but just out of reach. Now the dam is fenced off. Other life has gathered momentum rapidly in and around the new body of water. Frogs breed in large numbers. Vulnerable at every stage of their life cycle, birds feed off them in large numbers. Kingfishers breed nearby, herons and shags fly in seasonally to feed when the weather over bigger water areas may be stormy. Rough grass and pond weeds protect enough of the little amphibians for us to be discovering them all over the block where cover exists, as they hibernate away from the water each winter. Ducks breed on the dam, both mallard and teal. All manner of insects—dragonflies, mayflies, gnats and more—breed in the water and act as further food supply. There are nights that are humid and warm, where a hatch occurs. Swallows can be seen busily feeding on the clouds of whatever it may be, above the water. The acrobatic flights of these distinctive migratory birds continue well into dusk. At times other birds, such as fantails, will hover and dart over the dam's surface to feed. Flocks of goldfinch, yellowhammer and chaffinch feed from the ripening grasses that all through summer flourish along the banks. We have discovered small lizards down there as well as the many insects they need in order to survive.

The presence of cover attracts rabbits and hares, while

naturally enough a feral cat is attracted to a place where there are ducklings and other young birds to hunt. It would be possible to go on, but the point is made. The dam provides habitat. So, negative changes have also occurred. One further example is the increase in magpie numbers. We've seen that they raid nests, eating fledgling birds, while their natural aggression will drive away the song thrush who sings from the same macrocarpa trees those black and white predators claim as their own.

Enough conservation literature exists to make a case for the dam as a frog habitat, especially if, as we intend, native shrubs and trees are planted along the gully above and below the site of the dam. In fact, it will appear to be an act of conservation. The list of trees we are thinking of—manuka, flaxes, hebes, kowhai, maire, totara along with feed trees for kereru the native wood pigeons, tui and bellbirds—suggests a case could be made for ecological awareness. Of course, just like other plantings, there is no guarantee that ours will survive. We've had other years when losses through drought have been close to one hundred percent. If that happens, we will just plant again.

Yet an intervention is an intervention. Are aesthetic reasons sufficient to justify this intrusion? Returning to the original question, is the dam a move back to nature, or a step toward the future? Moving into the future there are things we may need to acknowledge—including the notion that we cannot turn back the clock, or return to a golden age of balance and calm. In 1930 Charles Elton declared, 'the "balance of nature" does not exist, and perhaps has never existed'. What if any step into the future requires a step toward nature?

We are reminded by the Australian, Tim Low, that while 'we have engineered the earth to meet our needs, many other species find their needs met too': some species seize our meddling as an opportunity to breed successfully in environments that suit them also. If humans are removed from the planet because we fail as a species, that doesn't mean life will end. Spaces such as the dam, the life around and in it, may well continue. In what form will depend on how change occurs on the planet. Wendell Berry says:

> . . . we must learn to acknowledge that the creation is full of mystery; we will never entirely understand it. We must abandon arrogance and stand in awe. For I do not doubt that it is only on the condition of humility and reverence before the world that our species will be able to remain in it.

The fragility of a butterfly's wing in the face of the wind, or soaring of a hawk in defiance of gravity, the passage of light through water in the dam captured on film as reflections—do they indicate the future? Darwin beheld miracles and wonders that unlocked keys to what was then radically new thought. Yet he stood before that knowledge with the same ultimate limitation common to any person—a need to use words to communicate the story. When we read his words, our intellect may understand them, but our comprehension of the issues we face dealing with the natural world still seems curiously limited. When we harness our actions to economic outcomes, do we really feel we are being objective? Today we still persist with acting in largely unconscious ways, peering anxiously outward from our grove of trees to the savannah beyond—behind us monsters lurk in the dark forest, and to the front of us stretch vast predator-populated plains. We stand naked before the depths of our thought processes, adult maybe, but with childlike emotions twisting our insufficient knowledge askew.

Last year three different pairs of ducks used the banks of the dam as a nesting site. One pair, a mallard drake and khaki Campbell crossbred female, successfully fledged twelve ducklings from thirteen hatched. They have arrived back at the dam to winter over. I've no idea where they have been for six months, and to be truthful didn't expect them to return. This brood has also survived the shooting season that occurs during late autumn where I live, in a tiny settlement at the edge of the hills. Most ducks are lucky to actually keep a single duckling from a hatched sitting around here, where feral cats, hawks, eels, ferrets or stoats, as well as humans, carry out the role of predator. In about two months the pair will nest again, and we will see how they fare. From time to time Catherine has wondered about having tame ducks on the dam. It seems we don't need to bother, nature is going to provide.

Today low-angled winter sunlight streams through the window pane onto my back. It is good to be alive and warmed in this way. If I wish to pause for a rest, an easy turn has me looking westward through that same window pane to where the dam lies catching the light thirty metres away. Beyond the fence, sheep graze under the olive trees. The olives will be harvested tomorrow.

The forecast for tomorrow—fine weather, with frosts. The story of this place continues.

Harvesting the olives

This morning, I put on my raincoat and winter underwear, because today's olive picking weather is downright mean. A strong southerly is blowing through the laden trees, and their branches bend away from it. Underfoot, the grass is soggy, and the threat of more rain means getting on with the job as quickly as we can. Each branch, as we pull it toward us to pluck the olives, sends a shower of water down the arm of the picker.

Memory has the harvesting of produce taking place in warm dry weather. The long hours of work through summer are supposed to result in similar weather when it comes to gathering the crops and storing them away. But we have committed to getting the harvest to the press in Martinborough today. Other growers have booked the machinery for their own harvest, and it is a case of fitting in once the commitment is made. We have no option but to get on with the job.

After all, being out in the weather is a part of who we are. In 1990, while New Zealand celebrated one hundred and fifty years of nationhood, Catherine and I spent most of the year cycling overseas, through Italy, Switzerland, France, Ireland and England.

'You'll paint differently when you've seen some of the stuff overseas,' a woman had told me, at an exhibition opening not long before Catherine and I left for our trip. She was so sure of herself and her opinion. I am still not so sure that my painting changed because of the travel or the large number of wonderful art works I viewed in that time. Perhaps I was already set in my ways?

'If you get to Ireland you'll never leave to come back home,' my old friend Michael Harlow laughingly told me one night after a couple of glasses of wine. I laughed back at him. He has travelled endlessly and places didn't seem to tie him down. But what did I know? I was in my forties and hadn't even been over to Australia to visit two of my sisters and one of my brothers who all lived there.

We were just having a look, seeking out a way forward for ourselves as much as anything else—and were certainly outside in the weather. I had never been off these small islands of ours, so anything I did was going to be new and interesting. We landed in Milan and headed south into Tuscany, biking through weather typical of early springtime—rain, wind chill, and at times stunning sunshine.

Within the first week we were threatened with carabinieri, which cost us a summary fine of 70,000 lire that most probably ended up in a railway guard's pocket. My pocket was picked of 100,000 lire. I ran into a parked car while looking about desperately for toilets without really knowing what words I was trying to read on signs as we biked along. Arriving in Fiesole entailed a late-night bike ride on cobbled roads leading god knows where straight up a steep hill. There is a photo of me taken after three days on the road, and I look as if thirty years' aging took place in those three days. Then we left Florence heading south one sunny April day, had our lunch of crusty bread and soft cheese followed by an orange under olive trees off the road. The stress lifted, and we biked toward San Gimignano with the road open to us and anything possible.

For the next three months we cycled in Italy, a little in Switzerland, then in France and Ireland. Bikes are a great way to travel if there is no hurry. One moves quietly through the countryside—a place of sounds and smells as much as sights. There is the opportunity to jump off the bike and go to help a farmer get sheep into his barn for shelter, as we did one afternoon. I spent another day, in Ireland this time, turning heavy meadow hay with a pitchfork after seeing farmers working against the weather in a hedge-rowed field. At other times we saw wildlife we'd not have seen from a car or bus; once a fox burst across the road which, at that point, bisected woodland. There were many shrines and small gravestones along country roads in Italy and France. If we stopped to check, often enough the dates written on them were between 1939 and 1945. There were so many reminders of war, ranging from the English regimental banners that line cathedral and church walls, to a bunch of flowers placed recently by one of the small plaques we so often passed.

East of Florence, off the Appenine mountains down toward Faenza, we biked into the scooped-out valley along a road overlooked by bluffs into which great gun emplacements were situated. Like the hungry maw of ogres that the hills may hide, the fortifications made me wonder what it would be like to advance into such a heavily defended line of battle. It was near Florence that an uncle of mine was wounded by a landmine after only a few days in action, an event that saw him invalided home after years of training to fight. We biked through that countryside squandering days, taking pleasure in the beauty of springtime. It was a good place to be alive, yet we travelled over the bones of soldiers whose lives were lost through centuries of campaigns, campaigns that gained nothing for the victors to take with them when they in turn finished their lives. History makes a mockery of fighting to conquer and possess.

In recent years young New Zealanders have travelled to

Gallipoli to realise similar thoughts. They go and stand on a beach where bloodstains once washed against pebbles and sand, reminding them that aspects of our nationhood have been formed by invasion of other countries for purposes of war. Each Anzac Day, New Zealanders, Australians and Turks remember a campaign that is purported to have founded their separate countries in one way or another. The funny thing is, only the Turks are celebrating victory.

Catherine and I biked eastward from that Italian valley, past Faenza, Caorli and Venice, until we arrived at Bibione, about one day's bike ride from Trieste. Kiwi soldiers had travelled pretty much the same path in 1945 using military transport. At Bibione we were welcomed by the Paron family. In 1943 an earlier generation of this family had helped Catherine's father, Paul, at great personal risk, when he was an escaped prisoner of war on the run after the Italian armistice. From there we biked into the mountains and spent the next weeks following as closely as possible the route he had taken as he escaped into Switzerland. He spent months walking through enemy-held territory in the Alps to arrive at Bormio, a village on the Italian side of the border with Switzerland.

We spent weeks on our bikes, taking each day as it came, not knowing where we would sleep when night fell. I grew up secure in the mythology that New Zealand hospitality was something special, and that of the West Coasters, a step above that again. I hadn't expected the hospitality we received from Italians. Away from the cities, we met with particularly generous people. More than once we left a home into which we had been welcomed with something to eat and drink for the next day. Opening the daily journals I wrote, it is easy for me to once again feel the warmth we encountered, and the experiences that crowded in on us day after day.

Tuesday 1 May 1990

This morning Cesare took us to 3 houses that Paul hid in, while he lived through malaria and the presence of SS troops downstairs. We met Gino who was 17 yrs old at the time—such a warm person. It's very hard to try and breach the confines of our imagination and envisage what life was like in those times. In one house, 40 members of the Paron house were crowded, while Paul & Martin Hodges were hiding out in the hay barn above the livestock. In another, where a senile 91 yr old countess now lives, he was in the attic, very sick, while troops were billeted downstairs. He was shifted from house to house in the district for 4 months before having to go and hide in the mountains. In this region he is remembered with great warmth, and Catherine was welcomed as his daughter, without question. So many of the adults of that time are now dead—the names trip the tongues of widows and survivors—il morte, time and again.

Details become obscure, but the hay barn in which Paul hid the night he escaped is still standing. Though trees may have been removed or died, roads and houses modified—memory persists.

Friday 4 May

. . . last night Edo, our host, talked of being a partisan. He hates the Germans first, because as Don Luigi said—they are unpredictable, one day they'd shoot indiscriminately, the next laugh. Plus they had a vicious streak. Next the English—because they would not share. Next Mussolini—when he was a prison guard, the prisoners with the benefit of Red Cross were better fed than he was as an Italian soldier.

... Edo was saying in 1926, 4000 people lived in Castelnuovo del Friuli—milking cows and all sorts of traditional curios—he has a room devoted to all manner of tools, axes, saws, clogs, and so on, out of his past peasant way of life—but anyway—now 1,000 live there. The pastures have reverted to forest which is infested with goats and deer. The population has drifted to the USA, Canada, Australia and Argentina. He is sad that the sense of community is failing. He showed us his collection of 40 caged birds, finches, quail, and others. It was dark & they were tucked up for the night.

Monday 7 May

... but yesterday went on & on & on—until finally we found a hillside in Vodo di Cadore. The family closest, a young couple, took pity on us, so we ended up having a fine spaghetti, a heaped bowl of strawberries dressed with lemon & sugar; and of course excellent wine.

Wednesday 9 May

... Cortina, the camp didn't charge us at all for staying two nights. They said—'On bicycles, is gratis.'

... after setting off this morning there was a steady climb away from Cortina followed by 17 kms up-hill without a break to the Passo Falzarego at 2105 m. We had lunch there after 3 1/2 hours biking through sun/rain/and cold wind ... with snow around a lot of the way. A steep descent of 14 kms and here we are.

... Tomorrow—up and over Passo Pordoi 2239 m.

There is little doubt that we took our parents with us on our travels. Flying in dog-tired after travel from Auckland, over the terracotta-tiled rooftops of Milan, I had no idea how much the point would be driven home by the coming months. Travelling through Italy made me see in new ways the price of the comparatively itinerant railways lifestyle my family had lived. We spent a night with the Mecchias, who helped Paul escape into the mountains beyond Spilimbergo during the war. Generations of the family have occupied the same house. There were other things, such as a concert of regional youth choirs at the Theatre Puccini in Merano, a resort and spa town tucked into the Italian/Austrian Alps of Sud Tyrol.

Saturday 12 May [1990]

... the local choir walks in and starts singing Verdi's 'Va Pensiero', one of Mum's favourite operatic choruses, the beginning of half a dozen full-voiced enthusiastic renditions of well known choruses. So I'm sitting in the box seat on the other side of the world, with tears in my eyes because something can be so wonderful—Verdi wrote for Italian voices and their full-throated emotion, and a choir of teenagers taught me the truth of that tonight—I wept out of sadness too, that has crept up on me over a while, how Mum & Dad brought us up to love so many things; art, music, ideas—and then taught us that nothing like that could be reached by any of us. Yet, so much can be gained by really going for it! Even if you cross the world to find out what Verdi can sound like without the help of a record player, or what Rembrandt looks like without the help of photography ...

... tomorrow night is a performance of La Traviata at another theatre—we will go to that.

223

Travelling across Italy was tiring, but not only for the physical effort. Being a long way from home and the familiar, allowed—or perhaps prompted—me (and Catherine, I think) to put thought into how we lived and what was important. In a way we were each putting all manner of experiences and family stuff into new context. Neither of us had imagined we'd be riding round Italy on bikes. Even now I'm not sure where that notion came from.

'Travel is not something I'm interested in. Y'won't catch me wasting my time travelling,' Catherine remembers me telling her, at Dunedin Library where we both worked long before we got together. Yet, there we were. My heart ached with the thought that my mother had never been to hear an opera, which she would have loved to do. And here I was, the least musical of the family, in a theatre in Italy listening to an old favourite, only four short years after Mum had died. I wasn't even able to tell her. Another thing I was unable to tell her was that, as we travelled through the spring months, roadside irises seemed to follow us, appearing on embankments, at gateways, growing wild, or in gardens, their spring blooms opening along with our schedule. I remembered how each time we shifted, her bulbs and iris corms would be wrapped once again, thoroughly damp, in newspaper. At the next garden she would dig a spot for them. Mum could grow just about anything it seemed—she'd just stick stuff in the ground and up it would come to flower or produce leaf where none was expected.

We passed into Switzerland.

Saturday 19 May. Zernez. Wine has become expensive, as has bread, but other food doesn't seem too unreasonable. One day soon we'll have to have another look at our finances and see if we can still afford to do such things as we did this morning and spend francs 7 on a tiny cow bell, or maybe a goat bell, as Cath says—'for when we get our own animals'.

224

Everyone that goes to the show today has paid for a ticket—with a 2 yr old Brown Swiss heifer and her calf as a prize. She is lovely, and we're told, worth 5000 francs. An absolute fortune.

By 19 May we had been on the road since late March and had travelled through Italy to Switzerland. There we stopped following Paul's tracks, and biked into France to go our own way, or so we thought.

In a little café in Paris, a tired trio of Greeks were playing in a desultory manner.

'Any chance of you playing some Theodorakis?' I went up to them and asked, after a glass or two of wine.

Their response was to perk up at once. Hell, someone was listening to them after all. After a short talk among themselves, they started playing. In a little café picked at random for our evening meal, I sat and listened while some hack Greek musicians working through another night away from home did indeed play Theodorakis. Their first choice instantly returned me back home. On the night my mother died, the cloud and rain cleared for a few moments, and the July full moon shone down on the snow-covered slopes of Mount Taranaki. It was just after two a.m., and the music on the record player was Theodorakis—the same tune I listened to now in a Parisian café. One tune after another they played, and we let them see our appreciation. What a night.

By way of France, Ireland, England and Canada we returned home, arriving in September. Even in Italy we had seen a lot, and there was a lot more to come, yet a subtle shift had occurred—our plans on returning home were beginning to form. We would be biking along in Ireland, say, and get off our bikes to look at a dolmen, or a dry-stone beehive hut built perhaps five thousand years ago—an hour later back on our bikes we'd just as likely be talking about what we could do when we eventually arrived back home. Living in Auckland no longer seemed an attractive, or even viable, option. So often our bikes took us through small towns, fringe settlements, and we could see, smell and hear life in the country wherever we pedalled. After three years in Christchurch and the same in Auckland I was ready to taste fresh air once more, to let my hands ache from a day working outdoors. It was time to be building a new life, and planting ourselves as well as trees.

I reached a stage where I was enjoying being away, but ready to be home and getting on with life. At no stage did I imagine my experience would be similar to that of a friend from years before. Tim was a superb potter when I knew him, and maybe he still is. It is difficult to imagine what he'd do with his time if his wheel was still and the wet clay absent from his studio. One day he told me about his return to this country.

'A mate and I were hitching round Japan,' he said. 'All we had was our clothes and a jar of dope. It was all part of the hippie trail thing, through South East Asia following poppies, that sort of thing. That's why I left Auckland in the seventies. We were just bumming round, not heading anywhere. One night we needed a place to sleep, so we knocked on the door of what looked like an old monastery. The door was opened. "What took you so long to come?" the old monk asked, letting us in.' Tim told me he stayed there for twelve months. He became a student of the old monk, learning how to throw pottery on the treadle wheel, secrets of glazing, traditional patterns, the routine of meditation and hour upon hour of quiet. Then somehow it was time to decide if he was staying for the rest of his life, or getting the hell out of there, he told me. 'So, I contacted the family back home, borrowed money for an airfare and took off. That was okay.'

Pausing for a sip at his beer, he took his time rolling a smoke. 'Y'know Pat . . . as the plane circled over Mangere to come in for landing, I looked down, over the corrugated iron roofs of the city. They were so . . . oh fuck! I knew it then, mate. I made the wrong choice. The biggest mistake I've ever made was to come back.'

'Can't you go back to the monastery?'

'No money,' he replied. 'The kids, pottery, mortgage . . . no. Can't go back.'

As it happens, when Catherine and I returned, I was glad to be home. What's more, we were ready for the next step, together. After two years of looking about, we put money into the ten-acre block at Gladstone. Was it because of the travel that we moved from Auckland? I have no idea; we just acted as if there was no tomorrow and set about our plans without delay. Not long after we got home we bought a black and white sheep dog, Bess. She travelled with us as we looked for land. Perched on the back seat of our car, she couldn't wait to be let out if we stopped anywhere she had room to run.

Our imminent departure from Auckland seemed to polarise friends. The lawyer who did our land transaction paperwork was delighted for us. She was quite prepared to travel halfway across Auckland for red wine produced by Gladstone vineyard, and envisaged us planting ten acres of pinot noir, or chardonnay, spending days in the sun drinking the profits. A friend who grew up around Masterton was horrified. According to her we were heading back past the proverbial black stump—a point beyond which civilised people did not sleep at night. Someone else was at pains to let us know it was the most snobbish place in the country, with a surplus of private schools. None of them was accurate, although all of them had elements of actuality for us as we settled in the new place.

We planted grapes, but only about fifty vines to see how they went. Late frosts dealt to the early buds, while drought withered the growth that survived. We nursed them through a year, with buckets of water carried from the dam during the dry of summer. They were stronger the second year. We went away for a week at Christmas. The electric fence failed, and our yearling bull got in among the grapes. When we arrived home, I saw him lying, chewing his cud in the 'vineyard', his big body splayed luxuriantly over some now crushed grape seedlings. He'd finished off the leaves and trampled what was left. Sadly, I never did harvest a vintage of quality pinot noir. It was time to try another tack. Grapes could be someone else's problem.

Here in the Wairarapa, there is a hint of the Mediterranean. A number of winemakers have produced quality wine, and vines are an established feature of the landscape. I can look out to a vineyard from my study window, and recall seeing similar sights from the seat of my bike while travelling through Italy. In places we passed through, such as Faenza, and the Appenines, or across the Po delta, the New Zealand division fought its way across Italy. They became experts in wine— often drinking large quantities of the stuff, apparently, if opportunity presented. Abandoned cellars, once discovered, had their bottled contents dispatched with enthusiasm.

Another memory of the campaign, which occurs often in memoir writings by returned soldiers, is of the fighting that took place in olive groves. On Crete, the New Zealand forces used them for cover as German paratroops dropped from the sky. The Allied retreat took place through olive trees until the mountain roads were reached. In Italy they would feature again. And now, in the Wairarapa olive groves are becoming a significant element in the local economy, alongside the production of prize-winning wines. There are no battles requiring gunfire, although it will not be too long before water becomes a commodity to be fought over.

When we decided on growing some olive trees to see how they went, the idea was far from innovative. It was rather, just getting on with the same thing other people we knew were doing. That doesn't mean to say there was no thought in the project, or expectation. I even wrote poetry on the subject, although the reality had to be more pragmatic.

Olives happened to come available from Waimea Nursery in the Nelson area. Because of an oversupply problem they were going cheap, so we bought about one hundred and fifty trees to plant. For pollination purposes there had to be more than one variety, so we settled for various types—koroneiki, picual, leccino and frantoio, then Hardy's mammoth—we already had one or two verdale trees, and we tried some pickling olives named barouni. I transplanted a special little tree from an earlier planting, an El Greco. That little fellow never made the grade.

It never ceases to amaze me the number of ways trees can die. Take El Greco, for instance. When we brought him home from the nursery he was a sprightly young shrub, bright of leaf and sturdy. First he ran afoul of our chooks. They were let out to forage, and one of them decided it was okay to play with leaves that moved in the breeze. So El Greco experienced life in the rough for the first time and lost most of his foliage. Slowly he recovered, and sprouted new and tender leaves. A late frost dealt to that sign of promise. So there was the olive tree, a shattered set of twigs all summer long, and I was too busy to throw him away. In the autumn rains a miracle happened. El Greco came to life. New shoots sprouted from his tiny trunk. So we protected him from frosts all winter long. The next summer proved to be the mother of all droughts, and El Greco was not the only tree to lose his leaves. We planted one hundred hedging trees along a fence line, and lost ninety-seven of them. But El Greco came back with multiple shoots. We nursed him, and he grew through an uneventful year. The following year we had to shift plants we wanted to keep after subdividing the property. Of course the olive trees went with us. The next year El Greco began to look the part; he obviously enjoyed the transplanting, which was against the odds. Great, we thought, what a survivor.

The following year, for no reason that we could tell, he turned brown—a sort of bright rusty brown. Then he died. The next year no leaves sprouted. Stress, some people suggested. The frost does that sometimes, others suggested. How would I know? What I do know is that trees may be planted and some live, others thrive, and then again inevitably there are the ones to die—that is the way of it.

Anyway, we planted the new olive grove. Laid out in rows, six metres between the rows, five metres between each tree in a row, the small plants looked even smaller in the space of the paddock. Frosts took a few trees during the first winter, in particular the barouni we thought might be good pickling olives. Seven years on, we have our first harvest pressed and settling in the garage. It may be only seven litres, or six-point-nine to be precise, but we have managed to grow the trees, pick the olives, and have evidence to prove it. The product smells of fresh cut grass, and has a peppery aftertaste, and we're happy with that. Given an ounce of good fortune, over the next few seasons the harvest will increase and we will have surplus oil—but there is no point in anticipating results. One thing we have learned the hard way is how plans have a way of twisting and turning away from expectation.

Nothing in my childhood helped me toward this notion of staying put and reaping the harvest over long periods of time. When we first arrived at this place, I was expert at the quick fix and getting on with stuff, but had no knowledge of doing things that would last.

The olive harvest is heavy with the accumulation of memory, and stories of the world I carry within. Dad would look up from weeding a row of carrots, or straighten his back with a bag of potatoes in his hand, maybe bend to pick the season's first tomato then turn to say, 'the tilling of the soil is a noble occupation,' giving his characteristic chuckle at the saying he'd turned into a mantra.

There is another story he used to tell.

'You're a chip off the old block,' he would say, talking about my farm leased a fair while ago now, or the block we live on at Gladstone. 'I had my eye on a piece of dirt once. Down at Hampden, it was. A real corker really, sloping down to a creek for irrigation. It can get dry down there y'know. Beautiful soil. Deep and dark, it can grow anything. Yes, I should have bought that block . . .'

'Why didn't you?' I asked once.

'Oh well,' Dad paused. 'It was the Depression y'know, back then. My own mother, who owned the land, and Val, didn't think it was a good idea. Val and I had two of your sisters by then, and the railways were a secure job . . .' And, then there was the punchline, as always with Dad's stories of the past. 'Biggest mistake I ever made, not buying that place.'

My father made much of his regrets. He also taught us to long for things that were out of reach. There were his *Outdoors* magazines, and copies of *Field & Stream*.

'Canada is where I'd go,' he'd look up and say. 'The fishing in those lakes . . .' Once more I was allowed to feel, if it weren't for kids like me, one of my parents would have had a happier life. He'd have been a fishing guide in Canada. Untroubled by railways, the next shift or anything else, my Dad could have done what he wanted to do, which was hunt and fish. Without us kids in tow, his life could have been that of the artist Tom Thomson, except for the iconic paintings.

I read about the Group of Seven while working at Dunedin City Library. Their landscape painting, which dominated Canadian art for decades early in the twentieth century, was a tribute to wildness and used vibrant colour that impressed and influenced me. Any history of their work also deals with the painting of Tom Thomson (1877–1917). Thomson's small oil sketches, and dramatically curtailed life, appealed to my sense of the romantic. He lived as a fishing guide in Algonquin Park north of Ontario to make money so he could pursue his love of painting. His death is still a source of mystery nearly a hundred years later. He drowned, whether by accident or foul play is open to conjecture. In Vancouver on the last leg of our overseas travel there was, by chance, an exhibition by the Group of Seven and Tom Thomson. The Thomson oil sketches, often painted on the lids of cigar boxes measuring only 20.5 cm x 27 cm, were a particular inspiration to me, and live on in my imagination as a pinnacle of spontaneous expression. I had earlier fished for salmon, walked among mountain goats, seen elk—and hitchhiked through the Rockies. We got a chance to fly in a helicopter high over the mountains north of Vancouver Island, a wonderful but hair-raising experience.

I could feel the presence of my father, yet returning home I never talked with him about what I'd seen. Somehow it seemed important to leave his dreams and lamentations intact and undisturbed. He was too old by then to go anywhere, and I realised that sometimes people need their unattainable dreams to maintain their day-to-day existence. Achieving the dream may be an utter burden, a dose of reality that dashes all romance. I never showed him the stunning prints of Tom Thomson paintings that we bought, never tried to describe what it was like to paddle a traditional handmade Canadian canoe.

'How's the garden going?' I'd say when we saw each other.

'Oh,' he'd reply, 'the carrots aren't bad. It looks as if the beans should be good this year. They'll be late though.'

If the talk got close to fishing he'd just say for the umpteenth time, 'Oh, well the tide goes out too far from here to bother.'

For whatever reason, he chose to live out his last years in Stratford, many kilometres from the nearest beach.

Come to think of it, I seldom talk to my family about where I've been.

If I did, would I have said six months ago that rain falls on the iron roof and it may be the last sound we are conscious of before sleep arrives to dream us? My lover's body is next to me between the sheets, firewood burns in the grate where we sat reading earlier in the evening. Nights grow longer, and the focus is changing. Summer, with her long days spent working outside, has about ended. Last night ten millimetres of rain fell. After months, the dam is filling. Leaves are turning rusty red and gold on poplar and oak trees we have planted. Not long ago nuts lay on the ground ready to gather, mushrooms appeared overnight to be harvested. Then it is olive harvest. We woke to the sound of more rain.

There is always going to be more to record here than rainfall. We grow into and out of places, attributing stories as we go. Without the stories we seem to lack something fundamental.

Every detail has a story to it, no matter how inconsequential it seems to us as we pass by. The footprints of the heron that has waded round muddied edges of the dam for a few weeks now have been smudged out by the rain. That might end up a journal entry, just like the ducks that have flown in at dawn. We could hear them in the dark, and there'll be more of them soon. Shooting season started a few weeks back, but not on our dam. Tree planting starts soon—we are looking forward to that. Ken from next door has given us some miniature daffodil bulbs to plant under the she-oaks, chestnuts and pin oaks at the bottom of the drive.

Now I would have to say that, coming up the drive last night, I noticed Ken's bulbs are in bloom. The seasons have changed, just as I have.

I realise at last that, like Dad, I'm in love with the telling of stories, the language of place that occurs in the naming of olive varieties for example, names running like the scent of oil into a bowl beside crusty bread on the table—frantoio and leccino, picual or koroneiki, giving our place character while the trees grow. How could we plant an olive tree named kalamata without accenting a cadence of seasons in this place, filtered through stories of fathers who fought in the Greek olive groves not unlike these we have created? Who we are becomes not one but many words, with roots that spread back into the soil of a hybrid ancestry, where continuity is drawn from stories of many places.

Where we look down to the gully, even our planting of indigenous seedlings among self-sown plants is a story being lived out. Words are used to describe our actions, and again every time we name something. That most commonplace of all self-sown trees in our area, the lemonwood, might be valued because it grows anywhere, although some would describe it as a pest. The crushed leaves reminded early settlers of the scent of lemons, hence that name. It has a Latin name also, pittosporum eugenioides, which could provide another clue to its story if I had an aptitude for botanical terminology. And then Maori valued its scent, obtained from the sap, calling the tree tarata.

Learning the Maori names for trees such as rangiora and maire, horopito or horoeka adds a layer of recognition to our view from the windows. Even bird names are resonant when the bellbird can be korimako, a name with its own music. Each year the nomadic shining cuckoo, the pipiwharauroa, arrives to plunder a nest to serve as a foster home for its offspring. The little grey warbler, ririroro, serves as host.

It was Dad, and his playing with words, that awoke in me an appreciation of language. Are the failed dreams of the parent fulfilled by the child? The trees we plant seek out light, growing the best they can in whatever situation their roots find themselves. Not all of them make it. For all our gifts of language and reason, we are not very much different. We eventually have to seek out a place to be ourselves, and no matter how stunted or twisted, it is who we are. I look out from my study window at the olive trees now. They are planted either side of the drive in their rows, so that we pass through them when we arrive home. They lean away from the nor'west wind which is blowing today. To the north side of the house, native trees, nga rakau, form another pattern, one of variegated greens, in their leafy growth. It is springtime here, bringing fresh growth with the seasonal burst we have come to long for through the long nights of winter. The native plantings catch the sun first thing each morning, and glint in light down along the gully after rain, while in the grove olive trees extend their supple branches into the sky.

I am beginning to understand something about the planting we have done. The olives, planted in rows, yet each one differing in size and shape; the creation of little bush blocks, with their hidden corners—I have always thought somewhere in my land of buried hopes and dreams that there would be a time, once the trees grew a bit, when I would walk through them with Catherine, and at other times with grandchildren. While we do walk through them, noting change, and maybe giving a helping hand sometimes to a struggling seedling, the imagined visits from toddlers have not taken place yet.

Regardless of my concerns, the trees we have planted grow, or fade into oblivion, alongside substantial self-sown regeneration. The self-sown native seedlings in the gully are growing into small pockets of bush, coming to life with birds, and all the other small creatures—lizards, spiders, moths and that multitude of living things existing in leaf-mould, creatures in love with the shadows and mulch. The trees, needing photosynthesis, continue their search for light. The cycle is returning to the gully. That is the way it can be, with longing and belonging.

Select Bibliography

These books have influenced the contents of *How the Land Lies*.

Baker, J.A. (1967) *The Peregrine*. New York, New York Review Books (Reprint 2005).

Berry, Wendell (1981) *The Gift of Good Land: Further Essays Cultural and Agricultural*. San Francisco, North Point Press.

de Certeau, Michel (1988) *The Practice of Everyday Life* (S. Rendall, Trans.). Berkeley, University of California Press.

Dillard, Annie (1974) *Pilgrim at Tinker Creek*. New York, Harper and Row.

Dillard, Annie (1989) *The Writing Life*. New York, Harper and Row.

Eiseley, Loren (1957) *The Immense Journey*. New York, Random House.

Fukuoka, Masanobu (1978) *The One-Straw Revolution*. New York, New York Review Books (Reprint 2009).

Gaita, Raimond (1998) *Romulus, My Father*. Melbourne, Text Publishing.

Galvin, James (1992) *The Meadow*. New York, Henry Holt and Company.

Gornick, Vivian (2001) *The Situation and the Story*. New York, Farrar, Straus & Giroux.

Gray, Robert (2008) *The Land I Came Through Last*. Sydney, Giramondo.

Heidegger, Martin (1971) *Poetry, Language, Thought* (A. Hofstadter, Trans.). New York, Harper & Row.

Heuer, Kenneth (ed.) (1987) *The Lost Notebooks of Loren Eiseley*. Boston, Little Brown & Co.

Hunt, Janet (2008) *Wetlands of New Zealand: A Bitter-sweet Story*. Auckland, Random.

Jamie, Kathleen (2005) *Findings*. London, Sort of books.

Jung, C.G. (1965) *Memories, Dreams, Reflections*. New York, Vintage.

Jung, C.G. (1964) *Man and His Symbols*. London, Arkana (Reprint 1990).

Leopold, Aldo (1993) *Round River: From the Journals of Aldo Leopold* (ed. Luna B. Leopold). New York, OUP.

Leopold, Aldo (1966) *A Sand County Almanac: With Essays on Conservation from Round River*. New York, Ballantine.

Lopez, Barry (1988). *Crossing Open Ground*. London, Pan Books.

Mabey, Richard (2006) *Nature Cure*. London, Random House.

Nelson, Richard (1991) *The Island Within*. New York, Vintage.

O'Sullivan, Vincent (2002) *On Longing*. Wellington, Four Winds Press.

Park, Geoff (1995) *Nga Uruora: The Groves of Life*. Wellington, Victoria University Press.

Park, Geoff (2006) *Theatre Country: Essays on Landscape & Whenua*. Wellington, Victoria University Press.

Pollan, Michael (1997) *A Place of My Own: The Education of an Amateur Builder*. London, Bloomsbury.

Ruark, Robert (1957) *The Old Man and the Boy*. New York, Henry Holt & Co.

Sanders, Scott Russell (2000) *The Force of the Spirit*. Boston, Beacon Press.

Snyder, Gary (1980) *The Real Work: Interviews and Talks 1964–1979*. New York. New Directions.

Snyder, Gary (2007) *Back on the Fire: Essays*. Berkeley, Counterpoint.

Stevens, Anthony (1995) *Private Myths: Dreams and Dreaming*. Cambridge, Mass., Harvard University Press.

Suzuki, David (ed.) (2002) *When the Wild Comes Leaping Up: Personal Encounters with Nature*. Crows Nest, Allen & Unwin.

Thoreau, H.D. (1973) *The Illustrated Walden*. Princeton, Princeton University Press.

Wood, H.H. and A.S. Byatt (eds) (2009) *Memory, an Anthology*. London, Vintage.

Yanagi, Söetsu (1972) *The Unknown Craftsman: A Japanese Insight into Beauty*. Tokyo, Kodansha International.

Image Credits

Unless otherwise acknowledged, all photographs and art works are the work of the author.
E.J.M. McClure collection, Alexander Turnbull Library, p. 14.
White Family Archive, pp. 35, 45, 130, 131.
Henry Holt and Company, p. 120.
Kirkwood Family Archive, pp. 161, 174.

Acknowledgements

A number of people have contributed to this manuscript knowingly and unknowingly. To them I owe my thanks.

I would like to thank the Victoria University staff at Schaeffer House for the supportive environment they provided in which to study and work during 2009 when most of *How the Land Lies* was written. Particularly I thank my supervisor Chris Price with her smile and suggestion from time to time that I should 'dig deeper'.

Thank you to my fellow students of the 2009 MA (Writing for the Page), for their positive approach and shared insight.

The editing of Ginny Sullivan deserves a big thank you, for her positive approach and a job well done.

There would not be the same stories without my brothers, sisters and sons playing their part over the years.

To Catherine Day—thank you for your love, encouragement and enthusiasm.